Social protection and inclusion
European challenges for the United Kingdom

edited by Donald Hirsch

The **Joseph Rowntree Foundation** has supported this project as part of its programme of research and innovative development projects, which it hopes will be of value to policy makers and practitioners. The facts presented and views expressed in this report are, however, those of the authors and not necessarily those of the Foundation.

Published by YPS for the Joseph Rowntree Foundation

ISBN 1 899987 66 5

Prepared and printed by:
York Publishing Services Ltd
64 Hallfield Road
Layerthorpe
York YO3 7XQ

Contents

Foreword

Half a century after Beveridge, we still face challenges, both old and new, in ensuring adequate protection for those who are not sharing in the nation's rising prosperity. The old challenge is the persistence of poverty and want. One new challenge is the large increase in the number of households without income from work, many but by no means all of them headed by a pensioner. Another is the disintegration of the bulwark of plentiful and stable employment.

The UK government is not the only one to be wrestling with such problems, or considering radical reforms to its welfare state. Throughout Europe, there is fresh concern over the exclusion of groups who fall through the increasingly large holes in the post-war welfare net. Three years ago, the Council of Europe launched a project on Human Dignity and Social Exclusion, to improve understanding of the problem and build commitment to tackle it. The Joseph Rowntree Foundation has been happy to support this project as one of its main funders.

In 1998 the Council of Europe will be publishing the outcomes from the project and holding a major conference to disseminate them. This will give an overview of how poverty and social exclusion interact across the continent. But the Joseph Rowntree Foundation also wants to know what specific lessons the UK should be drawing from the European experience. In conjunction with the main project, therefore it brought together leading European experts for a seminar in York in May 1997. The seminar focused specifically on the issue of income protection.

In this short publication, Donald Hirsch has distilled the main messages for the UK that emerged from this expert discussion. In addition, the papers from country experts give a timely insight into how other countries are tackling the same social and economic trends as those that we are now facing, albeit from different historical and institutional starting points.

As with any comparative exercise, we cannot expect to import other countries' systems directly, but we can reflect on the values and attitudes that underlie them. The word 'solidarity' was discredited 20 years ago in Britain because of its association with militant trade unionism. Yet it still underpins social spending in most European countries, describing a commitment to inclusive societies in which a common protection against misfortune is seen as being in everybody's interest. Any welfare reform that fails to kindle that kind of attitude among the public at large is likely to be neither effective nor durable.

We hope this publication will be helpful in provoking debate and stimulating ideas on how the UK's new government can face up to the challenges of 'social protection' in the new millennium.

Sir William Utting,
Joseph Rowntree Foundation
November 1997

Part 1
Overview

1 European challenges for the United Kingdom

The United Kingdom is searching for a new strategy for protecting the vulnerable in society. Its government wants to promote social welfare and cohesion within tight fiscal constraints, and in ways that encourage active participation in society rather than passive dependency. These goals are common to most European countries. Two questions that will be asked frequently over the coming years are:

- How much are we willing to pay for social protection? and

- What kind of framework can gain the popular support and confidence needed to make it sustainable over a long period?

With respect to both of these questions, it is worth considering European norms. First it is interesting to know the extent to which taxpayers in other countries have been willing to continue funding relatively generous systems of social protection, at a time when the UK appears to have reduced provision relative to need. There is now pressure for similar cuts in other countries, but fundamental features of existing systems are being fiercely defended. This makes it interesting also to look at the second issue, the forms of social protection around which European societies have been able to cohere. The concept of social 'solidarity' that has built up around systems protecting people at all levels of society, and a new focus in Europe on extending this solidarity to newly marginalised or excluded groups, are highly relevant for the UK's future.

At an international policy seminar held by the Joseph Rowntree Foundation in York from 28–30 May 1997, a small group of leading experts from seven countries considered these questions against the background of a Europe in which a growing number of people face the risk of economic and social exclusion. The Foundation is the biggest contributor to the Council of Europe's project on Human Dignity and Social Exclusion, whose main findings will be disseminated at a conference in Helsinki in March 1998. The York seminar did not aim to produce a comprehensive analysis of social exclusion/inclusion across Europe, but focused on the contribution made by income protection, and on the lessons of other West European countries for future policy in the UK.

The present report starts by summarising some of the evidence that formed the backdrop to this discussion, by looking in the next section at trends in social need and social spending in the UK and some basic comparisons with other countries. The following section then discusses some of the main insights that emerged from the seminar, and draws general conclusions. More detailed descriptions of developments in each country participating in the seminar can be found in briefing papers that form Part 2 of this report.

THE VIEW FROM THE UK

In changing the terms of support for the unemployed, reviewing the structure of pensions, looking at how all statutory services can be made more efficient and effective, and in

Donald Hirsch, international adviser to the Joseph Rowntree Foundation.

a number of other ways, the Labour government appears to be seeking a form of state assistance that meets modern constraints and goals.

The spirit of such change is not all new. There is a continuation of the agenda of the previous government of containing the overall level of public spending, reducing avoidable dependency and considering where private financing could replace or complement the contribution of the state. But Labour presents its mission as more than just trimming the welfare state. It retains a more specific commitment to social justice than the previous government, and wants to find ways of building social cohesion. A long-term objective must be to rebuild public confidence in the way money is spent to meet social needs, and thereby to create a stronger political commitment to fund such spending adequately.

These problems are not unique to the UK. Many of its European neighbours are currently having to ask whether they can afford to maintain generous systems of social security that they have built up since the Second World War. In all countries, rises in the numbers of unemployed and retired people over the past two decades have coincided with political and economic constraints on levels of taxation, of social charges on employers and of public borrowing.

Five aspects of the UK's situation

Five aspects of the UK's situation are particularly striking:

- a rapid growth in the number of households that lack access to income from work

- a relatively modest growth in the biggest of these categories, retired people, over the next 20 years compared with other European countries

- a decline in the relative incomes of those depending on state benefits in the UK over the past 20 years, together with an increased amount of means-testing

- a growing amount of inequality both before and after redistribution

- a stabilising of the proportion of national income taken in taxation in the United Kingdom, at a time when in other countries it has been rising.

One interpretation of this evidence is that, over the next ten to 20 years, the UK has the opportunity to create a more robust system of income protection without courting economic disaster, providing that support can be built at a political level to pay for such protection.

More households lack income from work

As a society grows richer, it might be thought that fewer of its citizens will need to have their incomes protected. Yet, in recent decades, an underlying pressure to expand social mechanisms to transfer incomes has resulted from a growth in the proportion of households that cannot support themselves through earnings from work. As shown in Figure 1, the increase in demand on social security has come to a large extent from retired people, but also from claimants who are not working because they are sick, looking after children or unable to find a job. Today, there is one working-age person claiming benefit because they do not work for every two pensioners, compared to a ratio of one to five in 1971.

Figure 1 Non-working benefit claimants, 1971–95

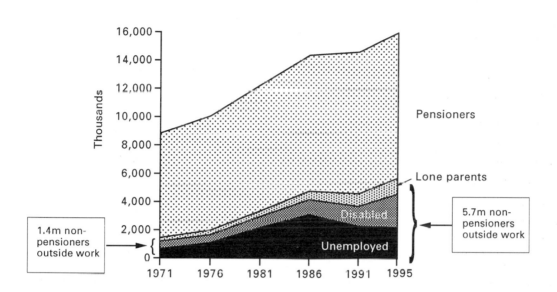

Source: Berthoud, R., Herbert, A. and Burghes, L. (1997) *Dependence and Independence,* Policy Studies Institute.

In recent decades the characteristics of non-workers in our society have changed fundamentally. Fifty years ago the great majority were wives, sons and daughters of working men, and received their income as within-family transfers. Today, the majority are workless heads of households or their dependants. Although not all of their income needs to come from the state (many retired people already rely on private sector pensions), society is bound to take a closer interest in ensuring that they are adequately provided for than in the case of family dependants of workers. This does not mean that state support will be provided unconditionally. The options presented in the government's New Deal on welfare to work attempt to ensure that everyone plays an active role in society, even those who

are not wage earners. Families have done the same for centuries. But it would be highly optimistic to assume that such policies will get so many people into paid employment as to reverse the underlying rise in the proportion of households without primary earners.

There will not be much growth in the number of pensioners for the next 20 years

By far the biggest category of households requiring some form of income protection remains pensioners. In 1950, about one in nine British people were aged over 65; now it is one in six; by 2040 it will be one in four. But this very long-term change will be particularly gradual over the next 20 years. As shown in Figure 2, the ratio of people of working age to retired people will fall in the UK from three to two-and-a-half by 2020, but this fall is modest compared to other countries. Because of an earlier ageing of the population, the UK presently has lower 'support ratios' than most other countries (compare the white bars on the graph), but by 2020 it will have more favourable ratios than in a majority of the countries shown (that is, the vertical dotted line is to the right of most black bars).

This slowing in the pace of demographic change potentially gives the UK more room for manoeuvre in the coming years – the more so because there is also a significant slowing in the growth in the number of over-85 year olds who make the greatest demands on health and care services. As discussed in the Joseph Rowntree Foundation's guide to the welfare debate (Hills, 1997), the growth in needs over this period will

not be so rapid as to make a general curtailing of entitlements inevitable. There is an opportunity to make real choices about priorities, both in terms of spending on various services and in the trade-off between public spending levels and taxation levels that are considered acceptable.

More means-testing, lower relative benefits
At the same time as more people are relying on state transfers because they lack primary income, the nature of this dependency is changing. First, there has been a particular growth in means-tested benefits (Figure 3). This has occurred mainly because of a growth in the number of workless people who have exhausted other benefit entitlements or whose entitlements do not bring them up to a means-tested

Figure 2 Projected support ratios in 13 countries

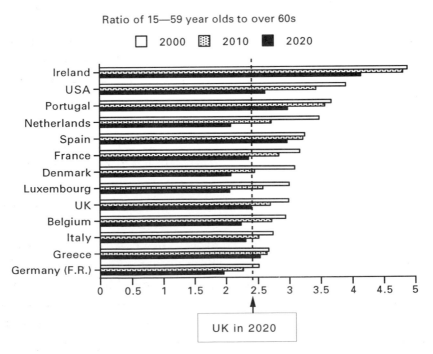

Source: United Nations (1992) *Economic Studies No. 3*

Figure 3 Real social security spending in Great Britain (1994/95 £ billion)

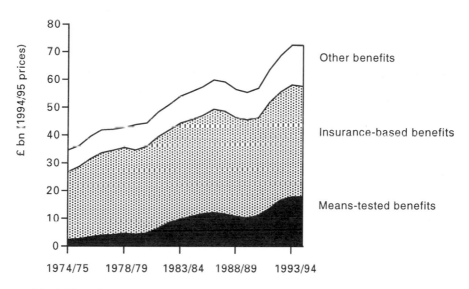

Source: Department of Social Security

threshold. Means-tested benefits grew by over seven times from the mid-1970s to the mid-1990s, and an astonishing 30 per cent of the population now lives in households receiving some means-tested support, far more than in other European countries.

The growth in means-testing does not just represent a rise in dependency, it signifies a steep rise in relative poverty. People dependent on the main social security benefits, means-tested and otherwise, have faced a sharp fall in living standards relative to the rest of the population since 1981, when most benefits stopped being raised in line with earnings and were frozen in real terms. The result is that benefits have declined by between one-fifth and one-sixth in value relative to average incomes in the past 15 years, for example from 34 per cent to 28 per cent of average personal disposable income for a single income support claimant (Figure 4). The fact that this policy is not generally being followed elsewhere in Europe

accounts for a large degree of divergence between the UK and other European social protection systems in terms of their adequacy.

Growing inequality
Inequality has greatly increased in the past two decades, roughly cancelling out the previous four decades of narrowing (Joseph Rowntree Foundation, 1995). This means that, insofar as welfare aims to protect living standards relative to the average, it has a much greater task than in the late 1940s. In practice, inequality in final disposable incomes has risen by a similar amount to inequality in original incomes. Internationally, taking a standardised measure of the proportion of households with half the average income, the United Kingdom is not exceptional in terms of the inequality of 'original' incomes (that is, before state transfers), but corrects for it far less than other European countries (Figure 5).

Figure 4 Income support and pensions relative to average personal disposable income (%)

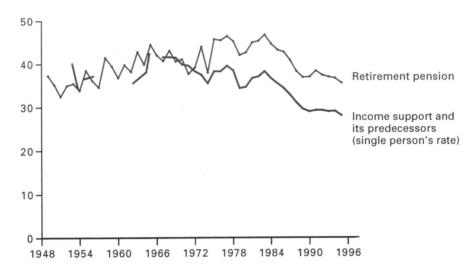

Source: Hills (1997); ETAS; Social Security Statistics; Evans' chapter in *State of Welfare* (forthcoming)

Figure 5 Inequality and its reduction: % of households with below 50% average income

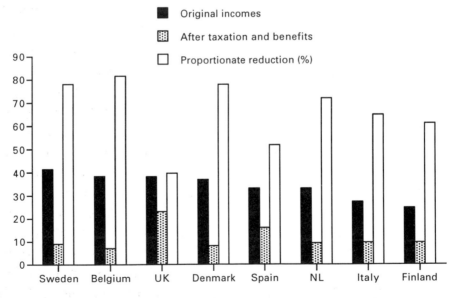

Source: Ditch, J., Barnes, H. and Bradshaw, J. (1996) *A Synthesis of National Family Policies 1995.* European Observatory on National Family Policies, EC, Table 4.4

The UK tax haven?

Successive UK governments since 1976 have shown a strong-willed determination to contain public spending, and have done so rather effectively relative to other countries. They have not shrunk the share of the state in GDP, but prevented it from growing over the long term. As a result, the overall tax burden has not gone up, as it has in most other countries, including both low-tax ones like Japan and high-tax ones like Denmark. The result is that the UK has gone from being a medium-tax country in European terms to imposing a lower relative tax burden on its population than any other European Union country except Greece. These comparisons, shown in Figure 6, emphasise just how much variation there is in the share of income that people in different countries are willing to devote to public purposes. Although income protection and redistribution are not the only functions of public spending, differences in tax shares can be explained to a considerable extent by the generosity of social security spending, which in

the UK is easily the biggest item of public expenditure, accounting for around a third of the total.

Payment choices ahead

Taking these five trends together, it is evident that the UK is catering less generously than in the past for a growing number of households in need of some form of income protection. It is doing so to contain public spending, and in anticipation of further growth in demands. Yet helped by this prudence and by relatively favourable demographic trends, the UK will, on present policies, find it easier than its European partners to make the budget sums add up over the next 20 years.

One urgent question is whether it is acceptable to freeze indefinitely the real incomes of people who depend on benefits. If this policy had been followed since the 1940s, the basic retirement pension would be worth half what it is today. Even if second-tier pension provision improves, there will still be an issue of where to set the basic safety net. Income support was designed to provide subsistence, but most of its recipients depend on it for survival over lengthy periods rather than just to meet basic needs on a temporary basis. Of the six million households who claim income support, four million have been doing so for more than a year.

If people in the United Kingdom wish to retain a reasonably generous system of social protection, is there any economic reason preventing them from doing so? There is considerable agreement among economists that voting for marginal increases in the country's present low tax rates would be a political decision that would not put competitiveness in danger. The key question is, therefore, how such

Figure 6 Tax shares in selected OECD countries: general government receipts as a percentage of nominal GDP

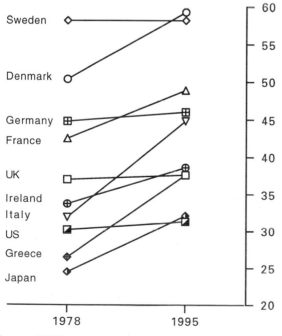

Source: OECD

9

political consent could be gained. There is not the same degree of general public support to spend more on social security as there is on items such as education and health that are perceived as affecting 'middle class' interests. The following discussion of the European perspective reveals an important difference in philosophy in this respect between the UK and most continental countries. In the latter, social security is seen as part of a protection system that benefits everyone, rather than just helping the worst off.

THE VIEW FROM EUROPE: A SUMMARY OF PERSPECTIVES FROM THE YORK SEMINAR

Social cohesion and fiscal crisis

Can European countries afford to maintain the generous systems of social security that they have built up since the Second World War? Growing demands on these systems, caused for example by rises in the numbers of unemployed and retired people over the past two decades, have coincided with political and economic constraints on levels of taxation, of social charges on employers and of public borrowing. Yet, while Europeans are gradually coming to accept the need to prune and to some degree to restructure social spending, they retain a strong belief in the importance of inclusive and adequate protection through publicly-funded social security.

Three main constraints are contributing to the fiscal squeeze:

- Europeans are unwilling to continue increasing the amount that they pay as individuals in taxes and social security

contributions. To a greater extent than the UK, many other European countries as well as Japan have felt able in the past 20 years to raise taxes to help pay for the rising cost of social protection (see Figure 6 above). But everywhere there appears to be some level at which a growing tax share becomes unacceptable. In Sweden, for example, the early 1990s saw a revolt against the growth of the share of the public sector to more than half the national economy (though not a drastic reduction in this share). France's fiscal crisis since 1995 has been based partly on the unacceptability of further tax rises.

- High contributions of employers to the cost of social security have in some countries helped make high levels of public spending less directly painful for individuals. But these employer contributions – which account for over a quarter of public revenues in France and Sweden, and one-fifth in Germany, compared to one-tenth in the UK – can themselves cause serious economic pain. In the light of high unemployment, they are seen as a threat to international competitiveness and to job creation. So the political pressure is to reduce or at least stabilise these charges.

- The degree to which the gap between receipts and spending can be bridged by public borrowing is severely constrained all over Europe. The most visible form of constraint has been the pressure to meet the Maastricht convergence criteria, that limit public debt as a proportion of GDP. However, macroeconomic pressures would in any case create similar constraints over the long term, since excessive public borrowing under liberalised world financial regimes can lead to unacceptably large increases in inflation or in interest rates.

A further important pressure, albeit specific to one country, has been the burden of German reunification. Social spending in the new *Länder* of Germany not only increases German social spending by the equivalent of 3.4 per cent of GDP (more than the total permitted public borrowing level under the Maastricht treaty) but also raises social spending in the whole EU by 1 per cent of GDP (see Chapter 2, Table 1). This gives some indication of the potential strains that could be created by an early entry of other central and eastern European countries into the European Union, which would make almost all the present 15 members into net contributors under the present rules.

What has so far been remarkable under these fiscal pressures has been the determination of many European countries to maintain what is considered to be an adequate level of social spending, and not to abandon the tradition of regarding that spending as an integral part of maintaining cohesive and stable societies. Reports of the death of European social democracy – for example in Sweden – have undoubtedly been exaggerated. As discussed in Palme and Wennemo's paper in this volume (see Chapter 6), Sweden has reduced and restructured some entitlements, but not fundamentally reshaped its system. Since the Social Democrats returned to power in 1994 after a three-year absence, the cost of reducing the deficit by 8 per cent of GDP has been met in

almost equal measure by higher taxes and by lower spending. In Sweden's political climate, the latter encountered more political resistance than the former.

When UK observers and decision makers consider the European view of social protection and its relevance or otherwise for our own future, it is worth bearing in mind on the one hand some principles and attitudes that underlie existing systems and on the other the ways in which countries are seeking to adapt to new circumstances without abandoning these principles. In this context, the following two sections describe some perspectives that emerged from the York seminar. These observations in no way constitute an endorsement of features of the systems described, or imply that they are directly transferrable to the UK. But before reflecting on the tension between pressures to draw from an 'American' or a 'European' model of social protection in the UK in the future, it is worth understanding some aspects of the latter that are not always well understood on our offshore island.

Three European attitudes

Social protection is for everybody, not a targeted minority
William Beveridge set the tone for Britain's welfare state when he spoke of slaying five 'giants': idleness, want, squalor, ignorance and disease. Even though the privileged middle classes have been demonstrated to be skilful at acquiring benefits from social spending, the welfare system has often been conceptualised as being intended primarily to address the needs of the most disadvantaged, the more so as time has passed. As the pressure to prune spending

has grown, the issue of better 'targeting' to those in real need has become more important. One result, in social security spending, is that the fastest growth is on means-tested expenditure, as described earlier in this chapter.

Elsewhere in Europe, the language is not of a welfare state to help the poor, but of a generalised system of social protection that creates 'solidarity' among different members of society regardless of how they fare as individuals. This creates strong income protection through the lifespan, ensuring that income does not drop excessively during non-earning periods. At one level, this 'solidarity' consists of mutual protection of people in particular occupational groups, with low-risk workers subsidising high-risk ones, without necessarily entailing redistribution between the lifetime rich and the lifetime poor. Work-based insurance systems are being called into question as work becomes less stable in European countries, and the adequacy of social assistance as well as social insurance is being reconsidered, (as described later in this chapter).

But even though they may need to adjust to new circumstances, these societies have not so far been drawn to the same degree as the UK into a 'targeted' view of welfare, because they do not think of collective social protection as being mainly for relieving poverty. An ordinary German who retires with a state pension worth 64 per cent of former earnings regards social security as a tool for organising a stable social and economic system, not as a way of protecting the poorest. His or her strong commitment to some form of collective pooling of resources to protect incomes gives a durability to that concept which may be more beneficial to the poor over the long term than targeted measures

based on transitory judgements about what level of poverty society is unwilling to tolerate.

Public insurance is not taxation
The bulwark of social protection in many European countries is provided through what the British would call national insurance and most Europeans call social security. The system initiated by Bismarck of employers and employees paying a proportion of income to build up various entitlements to pensions, out-of-work benefits and in many cases health care, accounts for a high proportion of public spending. But in countries like France and Germany, unlike in the United Kingdom, this form of insurance has been regarded as a system separated from taxation and 'state' (that is, central government) spending. Contributions are levied at given rates for specific purposes, and can be used only for that purpose. The only relationship with the state is that sometimes taxpayers have had to make up a deficit in social security funds; flows in the other direction are not permitted. (However, as Bouget demonstrates in Chapter 3, tax subsidies in France are becoming a larger and routine prop for social security expenditures, making the insurance–tax distinction less clear-cut.)

Such insurance systems have two big traditional advantages and one growing handicap. Their advantages are that they have produced connectedness and durability. Contributors can see clearly what they are paying for. As life expectancy grows, they can see the logic of a rise in contributions towards pensions. Moreover, because the insurance element is so clear, it will not be readily abandoned: it is seen as an essential part of modern life, just like insuring a car or a home.

There is a heavy resistance to the idea of providing such protection privately, partly because older people in these countries can still remember times of hyperinflation, and are disinclined to pin all their hopes on private investment. But the growing problem with insurance-oriented systems is that excessive reliance on contributory benefits leaves out a growing number of people as work becomes more fragile (as described later in this chapter). The need to provide for those excluded from or inadequately covered by insurance creates growing pressure to increase the role of means-tested assistance and other spending financed by general taxation. In such a situation, the connectedness of hypothecated insurance contributions starts to become diluted.

It is also worth noting, however, that another part of public spending distinguished in the public mind from that of 'the state' in many countries is local government expenditure. In Sweden, local authorities raise income taxes to run welfare services not provided through social security, including social assistance and education. The increased visibility gained from raising and spending this money locally helps sustain public consent for high levels of taxation.

Social protection is a shared responsibility
Part of the perceived 'solidarity' in European societies derives from the sense of a shared destiny, which obliges all to contribute to social protection. The most manifest form of this sharing is the contributions of both employers and employees to national insurance funds, and indeed the management of these funds by employer and labour representatives. In Germany, where the sense of social partnership is particularly strong, it is an important principle that each side should make an equal financial contribution to social security. The social partnership also stretches into other areas, including for example the organisation of worker training.

European societies are also starting to realise that social partnerships need to include more than just the two sides of industry. As more people are becoming excluded from traditional work structures, there is a need for a wider community partnership. The growing role of non-governmental organisations in a common fight against social exclusion was demonstrated in France recently by the formulation of wide-ranging legislation based on ideas by the ATD Quart Monde group (see Chapter 3). In Ireland, a national 'anti-poverty strategy' aims to bring together a wide range of actors (see Chapter 5). The strong voluntary sector traditions in the United Kingdom may in this area be an important example for the rest of Europe. But the efforts of this sector have hitherto been diffuse and relatively unco-ordinated. Effective social partnerships in the future may need to be more than simply the sum of many worthy but independent efforts to help the disadvantaged.

Three ways in which European social protection systems are having to adapt to new conditions

By protecting people marginalised by employment-oriented protection
Bismarck's idea of earning lifetime entitlement to social protection through contributions made when you were working was ideal for the immediate postwar period of near full employment. But recently, work has become

more fragile, and the number of working-age people who remain outside formal employment for long periods of time has grown appreciably. This creates a vulnerability and risk of exclusion for such people, particularly in countries where not just income protection but also health care entitlement is linked to public and employer-based insurance systems. In Sweden, tax-funded social assistance has always played a parallel role to insurance, to provide comprehensive protection. But in France and Germany, assistance has been conceived as a last-resort option, and has only recently attempted systematically to cover the many groups who are falling through the social security net.

These societies are not used to thinking about social protection as covering all residents or citizens – up until now, the 'socially insured' have consisted of those who have made contributions. The opposition in France to the Juppé plan, which was to a large extent based on linking social protection with citizenship and thus making it more universal, is a sign of how painful it can be to make such a transition. For those who have received favourable benefits from social insurance while paying relatively low income taxes, the options are not attractive. Either their entitlements need to be cut or their taxes need to be raised. In Germany, to the cost of high unemployment must be added the high transfers needed to top up the insurance-based pensions of people in the Eastern *Länder* to a level based on the Western protection system. There are parallels to be drawn between the new inclusion of those hitherto excluded by geography and those excluded by social or economic status. Instability in Europe is creating greater burdens on those in stable situations, who are having to pay not only for insurance

against risks to people like themselves, but also for an increasing number of fellow-citizens who find themselves outside the mainstream economy of Western Europe.

By giving greater recognition to work that is not full-time employment
A new form of protection based more on assistance for the excluded and less on insurance for those in the mainstream is highly unattractive to Europeans who have spent the past 50 years trying to build integrated and cohesive societies. A more appealing option in a world no longer dominated economically and socially by full-time employment is to broaden the routes to inclusion. Mothers who are outside full-time paid employment while bringing up children, people who care for elderly relatives, retired people engaged in voluntary activities, and many others, are all active in ways that are valued by society. Yet employment-based social protection systems have not traditionally recognised such activities as carrying value and thus conferring inclusion in mainstream social insurance.

To some extent, other countries can learn from the United Kingdom about giving recognition to these alternative forms of work more than the other way around. Part-time work and volunteering are certainly better established and accepted, and the benefits available to family carers have improved over recent years. People with certain home responsibilities are given national insurance contribution credits. But the degree to which non-employment activities confer entitlement to insurance benefit is less relevant than in other European countries, where the stakes are higher, since insurance-based benefits are so much more generous in relation to means-tested ones.

Some countries – notably central and east European – have for a long time given extra recognition to mothers who bring up children, crediting them with extra social insurance contributions as an acknowledgement for doing so. Germany too has now given contribution credits to those looking after children or other dependants. It has recently introduced a new system for recognising the contribution of people looking after relations who need long-term care, by allowing them to receive as cash a new benefit that would otherwise be spent on buying professional care services (see Chapter 4). European legislation has helped improve the position of part-time workers.

These are so far relatively small steps, but indicate a recognition of the need to adapt to a world in which the role of work has changed. The aim is to create conditions that encourage social inclusion and participation among those on the fringes of or outside the labour market, rather than merely protecting their incomes. Since work confers many social and psychological benefits, rather than just economic ones, income protection on its own can potentially be damaging, by sustaining people in a stigmatised position in which they do not make a recognised contribution to society. So a broader concept of inclusion will be a key ingredient in the future development of cohesive European societies.

By making realistic choices that address new needs at affordable cost
Europeans have been reluctant to accept a reduction in the generosity of any aspect of social protection. As France has found under both left- and right-wing governments, this

makes it difficult even to restructure a system at existing spending levels to meet new needs, let alone to cut it back to meet new fiscal criteria. However, one advantage of the earmarked nature of European social insurance is that some kinds of trade-off can be more visible and thus more feasible than under-pooled general taxation.

A straightforward example is pensions. In both Sweden and Germany, marginal cuts in the generosity of pensions have a greater effect on people who retire earlier. In Sweden, the cuts have been most severe for early retirement. A recent cut in German pension entitlements (from 67 per cent to 64 per cent of income in work) can be offset by those who choose to work beyond the normal retirement age, who receive a higher percentage. In both Sweden and Germany, one's (imaginary) account of public pension entitlement is translated on retirement into an annual pension based on years of remaining life expectancy. The message is straightforward: the pension rate is bound to be related to the ratio of working to retirement years; as life expectancy lengthens, people will either need to retire later, make higher contributions or receive lower retirement incomes. In the UK this principle is clear for anyone with a private personal pension, but much less visible to the individual in public arrangements or final salary based occupational schemes.

Another example from Germany is the new social care insurance described in Chapter 4. The biggest problem with introducing it was that social insurance in Germany has always depended on equal contributions by employer and employee, but any rise in already-substantial employer contributions could harm jobs. So a compromise was reached between employers and unions. The principle of equal contributions was maintained, but the unions agreed to abolish one day of public holiday a year, to offset partially the consequent rise in unit labour costs.

Welfare, work and competitiveness: the American or the European route?

The United States has always been known as a land of opportunity, but also of risk. European countries have had more stable social structures, in which the risk of catastrophe is smaller, but so is the opportunity to escape one's predetermined position in society. These stereotypes have become more relevant in recent years as what continental Europeans regard as the 'Anglo-Saxon' concept of flexibility has become more influential. These Europeans exaggerate the degree to which the UK has chosen the 'American' route: it has influences from both sides of the Atlantic. But they are right to fear that the globalisation of the economy is making it harder to maintain all aspects of European-style social protection, not least when at least one member of the European Union itself appears reluctant to agree to common standards.

It is beyond the scope of this report to analyse in any detail the social and economic advantages and disadvantages of American versus European strategies. But it is important to note that, in terms of their results to date, no one model produces ideal results (see Chapter 2). Quite clearly, the American model has enjoyed better performance in recent years in creating jobs and reducing unemployment, and hence one form of social exclusion. But its disadvantages are not just that it provides worse social protection for those who do fall by the wayside, but also that it is based on a low-skilled and unproductive labour market. Consider the following crude comparisons.

Figure 7 shows that the average member of the American population is still better off than the average European, but only because more Americans work, and for longer hours. Their income per hour is low relative to mean national income, so the average American must work harder to maintain an average living standard, and there are many workers in poverty who are

Figure 7 Productivity differences: US and EU

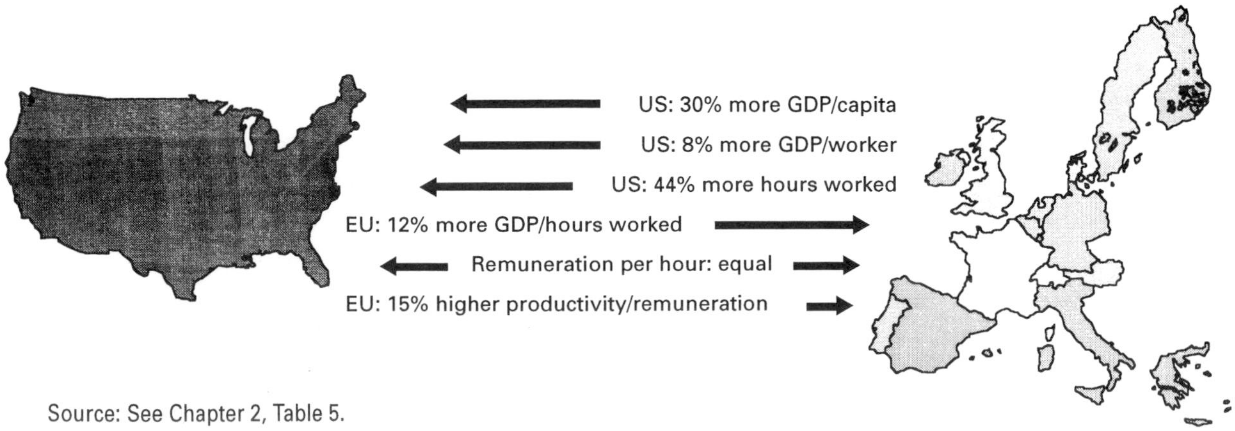

US: 30% more GDP/capita
US: 8% more GDP/worker
US: 44% more hours worked
EU: 12% more GDP/hours worked
Remuneration per hour: equal
EU: 15% higher productivity/remuneration

Source: See Chapter 2, Table 5.

on low pay. Despite a tax credit system that helps low-paid families, the American state does far less to reduce poverty than most European countries. On most measures its post-tax level of relative poverty is about twice as high even as the United Kingdom's (see for example Chapter 2, Table 3), which is itself considerably higher than most European countries (see Figure 5 in this chapter).

Conclusion – in search of a new social solidarity

The British have come to accept, more rapidly than most other European nations, that economic and social changes make citizens more vulnerable and inevitably reduce the protection of the old welfare state. They have also learned to live with greater inequality, and a reduced role for the state in counteracting it.

It would be foolish to pretend that the social protection systems of the UK's European neighbours provide ideal, transferable solutions. Even in those countries, social protection is unlikely to be sustainable in its present form. But there is now emerging a common European desire to create new forms of protection that maintain the principles of inclusiveness and social solidarity.

Will the UK participate in this social reconstruction? The British still appear to be more inclined than Americans to want the state to work towards a cohesive society that avoids the worst results of inequality and exclusion. There is reason to believe that over the next few years the political commitment to achieve those ends could grow. But this will not happen merely through a traditional swing in political mood back from 'right' to 'left'. It will need to involve the construction of new relationships between citizens and the state in which the majority of people feel that they have a strong stake in the form of social protection that is on offer.

References

Hills, J. (1997) *The Future of Welfare, A Guide to the Debate,* revised edition. York: Joseph Rowntree Foundation

Joseph Rowntree Foundation (1995) *Inquiry into Income and Wealth,* Vol. 2, Chapter 3. York: Joseph Rowntree Foundation

Part 2

Income protection and inclusion in European countries: systems, trends and issues

2 Western Europe: current practice and trends

Difficulties with a synthesis

It remains rather difficult to present a synthesis of trends in social protection development in West European countries in a well documented way. This difficulty has to do first with the limited comparative information that is available. Both the OECD and the EU Commission (Eurostat-ESSPROS) provide some comparative information. Yet this information is very aspectual, and is available only after some time gap. What is more important, however, is that this information refers to a traditional, system-oriented framework that is not very instrumental in providing a relevant assessment of policy trends and in locating basic policy shifts.

From 'systems' description to analysing policy change

Three perspectives may help to get social security out of its traditional 'systems' cocoon, and in that way contribute to a more relevant assessment of its development and of the challenges that confront it.

Beyond social insurance
A first perspective refers to the statutory and social insurance bias that has been associated with social (security) protection in the decades that followed the second World War. Both the Beveridge proposal and the continental systems that came under review after World War II focused on social insurance schemes by which the pre-war poor law and social assistance schemes could be made redundant. Yet the development during recent decades has reminded us of the intrinsic part which the latter continue to play in social protection policies.

Moreover, on top of the statutory – be it social insurance, social assistance or universal benefit – schemes we should take stock of any protection that is provided by occupational and fiscal schemes with respect to the needs and risks that are covered by statutory social protection. In line with Titmuss's social division of welfare, both occupational and fiscal welfare schemes should be taken into account as in fact they represent the hidden part of the building of social protection. These occupational and fiscal schemes, which also rely on collective decisions, contribute to the common aim of sustaining people's means by providing some form of replacement or adjustment income.

Social security in relation to workforce participation
A second perspective has to do with the isolated approach that is traditionally used in reasoning on social security policies. The latter have in fact focused for a long time on internal, endogeneous factors, thereby losing sight of the broader societal function of the social security system.

This function can best be explained by pointing to the basic societal process on to which social policy is grafted. It holds that we educate and train people to ensure that they are able to enter the (paid) labour market and thereby have the opportunity to gain a primary

Professor dr J. Berghman, Tilburg Institute for Social Security Research, The Netherlands.

income. And this income in turn enables them to have command over resources to guarantee their social integration. Yet, when this basic process is endangered because of limited resources that might prevent families from aiming at adequate education or training for their children, family benefits and study grants are activated. Moreover, when this process is interrupted because of unemployment, incapacity to work or old age, social protection systems operate to provide replacement income in order not to endanger social integration. Meanwhile restorative actions like health care, work mediation, retraining and even partial re-employment schemes are activated with an aim to secure a quick reinsertion in the labour market, restoring the basic process. When both these reinsertion devices and the income protection schemes are inadequate, however, the risk of social exclusion – of deficient social integration – materialises.

So social security systems basically operate as a by-pass mechanism in those cases where insertion in the labour force is no longer possible or desirable. In such cases their aim is to mend the chain by guaranteeing the availability of (replacement) income in order to safeguard social integration. Yet social security policies cannot limit themselves to the mere provision of income protection, be it at a minimum or at an earnings-related level. Income schemes have to be complemented – though not replaced as the OECD tends to suggest – by reintegrative actions like retraining, work mediation and rehabilitation schemes.

The fundamental importance of this basic societal process is shown by the way it helps define some of the basic models of the welfare state that are used to represent in simplified form some highly complex existing national systems. The traditional Scandinavian model emphasises (re)insertion in the labour market, whereas the continental/Bismarckian model stresses a good bypass mechanism with earnings-related benefits that are capable of replacing the lost wage to a high degree. The Atlantic/Beveridgean model focuses even later in the societal process by providing flat-rate income protection in order to safeguard minimum social participation; earnings-related protection was originally left to occupational provisions and private initiative. Southern Europe did not so much provide an intrinsically distinct model, but rather a less developed continental one.

In the 1960s and 1970s the countries with Bismarckian and Beveridgean social insurance approaches showed some convergence as the former included some generalised minimum protection measures into their earnings-related schemes whereas the latter introduced some earnings-related provision to complement their system of minimum protection (cf. Dupeyroux). In the late 1970s, however, this trend towards convergence was stopped and followed by a period of budgetary-inspired retrenchment policies (see below).

Social protection to protect society
Yet, the question remains why the function of income maintenance should be elaborated through 'social' benefit schemes. This is a third perspective. In the end, social and not just private insurances are used because it is society itself which tries to protect itself, internally, through obligatory schemes, against the dysfunctional effects of income interruption

which manifests itself with some of its members and beyond the command and the responsibility of these citizens. Citizens are encouraged by the government, and even obliged, to insure themselves against a number of social risks. And this is done, not so much to have the income situation of the citizens protected, but to prevent the latter from becoming a burden on the rest of society.

The effect of the income loss that is associated with the core social risks is in fact not confined to the person who is directly hit by it. It will reflect on others, even on to the broader society: from cultural and motivational effects on the children of the unemployed up to political instability and social upheaval. That is why nation-states try to protect themselves against the detrimental effects of the so-called social risks, why these risks may rightly be called 'social' and why they have to be covered by compulsory schemes.

Shedding post-war assumptions

In addition to these three perspectives that should inspire any relevant assessment of social protection development, three assumptions on which the post-war social insurance systems were based should be pointed out. The first was full employment (cf. the Beveridge Report): labour supply should be high enough to limit the number of the unemployed and to allow for the reintegration of those with a (partial) incapacity to work. A second assumption was that of the family responsibility of the insured worker. Benefits should be high enough to allow the worker and those who depend on his income, to live on. Hence, the introduction of derived rights and family rates (together with

child allowances). The family bias that was thus created could represent up to 30 per cent of the social security budget (cf. Meulders). Finally, there was the assumption of the typical industrial worker in a stable, full-time job.

These assumptions are important as they are opposed to the major challenges that have confronted the social protection systems in recent years. High unemployment rates have not just presented social security systems with rising numbers of beneficiaries and an ensuing expenditure growth but have also eroded their contribution base. Women's liberation and the growing labour market participation of women have not only diminished the need for family-based benefit devices, but the generalisation of the two-income family as the social standard has meanwhile brought single income households (and especially single parents) into greater risk. Atypical and part-time work represent a less stable basis on which to build benefit rights and urge the benefit schemes to devise more complex administrative procedures. On top of these shifts, progress in medical technology, the growth of life expectancy, the *de facto* decrease of the pension age (early retirement schemes) and the baby boom generation confront health protection and pension schemes with increasing expenditure figures.

Broad policy phases since the late 1970s

After the full maturation of the social protection systems in the 1960s and early 1970s one can distinguish three policy periods. A first one started in the late 1970s, early 1980s when the effects of the oil crisis and the economic recession of the mid 1970s fully materialised in growing numbers of beneficiaries and heavy budgetary pressures. This resulted in increased contribution rates, in cuts in benefit levels and in tightened eligibility conditions. Gradually this would enhance the legitimacy of the broad set of instruments that figures in the 'social division of social security'. Social assistance, occupational benefits and tax expenditure schemes were again discussed as alternatives to the traditional statutory social insurance schemes.

After some period of cutting, however, the awareness grew that no longer reducing the benefit levels, but rather redressing the growing number of beneficiaries had to be the target. This would lead to a second policy phase that was geared to tightening the influx of new beneficiaries and to speeding up their outflux, thus aiming at a smaller number of beneficiaries and hence a smaller budget load. Intensive retraining and reintegration schemes as devices of labour supply policies characterise this second phase, thus capitalising on the limited functionality of benefit schemes for the basic societal process.

Yet, at this moment, we seem to have entered a third phase. It becomes clear in fact that the scope of labour supply policy remains restrained within a context of limited labour demand. Hence, the basic social contract that implicitly defines the overall amount of labour demand, the way this is distributed, that primary and secondary income distribution are derived from it and that the value mixes of efficiency and equity, of work ethic and solidarity are called upon to underpin it, is being put on the agenda. At the same time the core social contract upon which social cohesion and stability rests is under scrutiny.

Trends in features of social protection schemes

Yet these periods as described so far rest on broad generalisations of the overall trends. But development materialises through incremental shifts in the different aspects of social protection schemes. The reports on *Social Protection in Europe* by the Commission of the EU provide an intelligent overview of these developments. Major highlights of them are that in all member states the share of GDP devoted to social protection has shown a significant increase since 1970. Overall, however, this increase has been curbed and the share has rather oscillated since the early 1980s (see Table 1).

These figures, however, are gross figures based on expenditures by the social protection institutions. Correcting them for taxes and social contributions that are levied on benefits leads to slightly different net figures (see Table 2).

With respect to financing, some convergence manifested itself in that, in countries like Denmark and Ireland in which traditionally general revenue was an important source of financing, the importance of contributions increased. With the exception of Belgium and The Netherlands, in the other countries, however, the importance of general revenue as a source of social protection financing tended to rise. Within contributions, some tendency to shift the burden from employers' contributions towards personal contributions can be seen. Yet, privatisation of social protection, although highly voiced in the policy discourse, and for which no general public support seems available, is far from being implemented systematically.

Detailed figures on the numbers covered by

Table 1 Total social expenditure as percentage of GDP, 1970–93

	B	DK	D	GR	E	F	IRL	I	L	NL	P	UK	E12
1970	18.7	19.6	21.5	–	–	19.2	13.2	17.4	15.9	20.8	-	15.9	19.0
1980	28.0	28.7	28.8	9.7	18.2	25.4	20.6	19.4	26.5	30.1	12.9	20.5	24.1
1985	29.3	27.8	28.4	15.4	20.0	28.8	23.6	22.6	23.4	31.7	14.2	23.8	25.9
1990	27.0	29.8	26.9	16.1	20.6	27.7	19.5	24.1	22.1	32.2	15.0	22.1	25.2
1993	27.6	33.2	27.6	16.3	24.0	30.9	21.4	25.8	24.9	33.6	18.3	27.3	27.7
			(31.0)										(28.7)

Note: figures between brackets include the new *Länder* of Germany.

Source: Commission of the EU (1995) *Social Protection in Europe – 1995*. Brussels – Luxembourg: Commission of the EU, p. 61

Table 2 Gross and net public and private expenditure for social protection (including health care) as percentage of GDP, 1993 (provisional figures)

	Gross public*	Net public	Private	Total
Belgium	27.3	n.a.	1.9	n.a.
Denmark	31.0	26.8	1.7	28.4
Germany	28.3	26.6	4.4	31.0
Netherlands	30.2	25.1	5.0	30.1
UK	23.4	23.2	4.7	27.9
Sweden	38.0	34.1	2.9	37.0
Japan	12.4	n.a.	n.a.	n.a.
USA	15.6	15.5	11.9	27.4

Note: * the provisional figures are based on OECD sources. The latter provide other information than Eurostat as OECD takes only public expenditure into account as it uses a broader definition of active labour market policies.

Source: Nederland – Tweede Kamer, *Sociale Nota 1997, nr 25002, 1 and 2*, p. 112 and further references

schemes are difficult to come by. As such, the scope of entitlements has hardly been changed. Indirectly, however, the growth of atypical labour contracts, targeting of benefit schemes and the (quicker) transfer of beneficiaries from universal insurance schemes to income- and means-tested, assistance-like schemes, a more intensive fight against social fraud and incentives towards reintegration have contributed to a limitation of the number of beneficiaries.

In the field of administration, some privatisation has been advocated as a means to increase its efficiency. This was explicitly the case in the UK and The Netherlands, but to a lesser extent also in Italy, Spain and Germany.

Adequacy of social security

In the framework of broader social protection policies in which preventive (labour demand) and reintegrative actions are of utmost importance, the social protection systems are being asked to guarantee minimum income protection (the Beveridge legacy) and to provide earnings-related income protection (the Bismarck legacy), in ways that do not counteract reintegration (the Scandinavian legacy).

Providing minimum income protection is beyond any doubt the primary task of the social protection system. Not fulfilling this task implies in fact that income poverty would continue to exist and that the necessary foundations on which to build any safeguarding of the acquired standard of living would be missing. Fully comparative evidence for all the EU Member States will become available only during the coming years. For the time being we can, however, for some countries and regions, rely on evidence that refers to the second half of the 1980s and that was brought together on the occasion of the first monitoring activities for the convergence recommendation. Table 3 and Figure 1 indicate that the poverty incidence that would exist without interference of the social protection system (before) is intensively reduced by the existing schemes (after). Even the least effective European system, that is, the Greek one, is doing a much better job than the US system. In this respect it is important to be aware that this effect is not solely the result of the formal minimum protection schemes but also of the aggregate effect of the entire social protection transfer system; that is, somewhat half of social transfers are directed towards households that do not need them to reach the

minimum level. At the same time the reception of social protection transfers by all sections of the population upholds public support for the schemes and in doing so also guarantees that the minimum income devices that are built into it retain their legitimacy.

Yet it would be short-sighted to limit social protection to a mere minimum protection. What should be aimed at in fact is to prevent people from sliding down to a situation at or below the minimum level. It is not by accident that panel analyses have shown that earnings-related, above-minimum protection is the major device that prevents households from sliding down to poverty and even to multi-dimensional deprivation. It prevents the majority of the elderly, of the disabled and of the short-term unemployed from sliding down to the minimum protection level, to poverty and further down to a situation of multi-dimensional deprivation. One example that points to the important mobility mechanisms that are at work is given in Table 4. It shows that the very stable numbers of the poor we find each year in The Netherlands conceal

Table 3 Poverty incidence before and after social security

	Before	After
NL	40	8
UK	45	13
US	38	25
GR	38	20

Source: Hausmann, P. (1993) 'The impact of social security in the European Community', in J. Berghman and B. Cantillon (eds) *The European Face of Social Security*. Aldershot: Avebury, pp. 109–21

Figure 1 Households with incomes below the poverty level, before and after social protection, second half 1980s

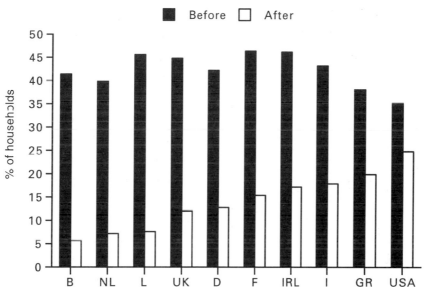

Source: Hausmann, P. (1993) 'The impact of social security in the European Community', in J. Berghman and B. Cantillon (eds) *The European Face of Social Security.* Aldershot: Avebury, pp. 113–14

remarkable processes of mobility in and out of poverty. In each of the years under consideration some 8 per cent of the population was in poverty. Yet, taking the three years together, as much as 15 per cent of the population was shown to be hit by poverty in at least one of the three years. On the other hand, only 1.2 per cent was in poverty throughout the period. With a view to monitoring, all this pleads for having poverty or deprivation incidence indicators replaced by some sort of mobility indicators. The analysis of odds-ratios over time is a first step into that direction.

Comparative information with respect to the effect of social protection on the income distribution may be scarce at cross-section level;

Table 4 Population in poverty (according to legal poverty line) in The Netherlands, 1986–88

		% of population	% of those poor in at least one year
Never poor		84.7	
Poor in at least one year		15.3	100
of which:	– in 1 year	7.8	51.0
	– in 2 years	6.3	41.2
	– in 3 years	1.2	7.8

Source: CBS (1995) as reported in Dirven, H.J. and Berghman, J., 'The evolution of income poverty in The Netherlands: results from the Dutch Socio-Economic Panel survey', *Innovation*, Vol. 1, p. 86

it is even more so at longitudinal level. Evidence for some better documented countries, however, points to the plausibility of rising income inequality and a growing dualisation of income distribution and social protection.

A Europe model?

The functionality of the social protection system can be assessed only in the framework of the broader labour-income nexus of which it has become an integral and intrinsic part. In this respect one is becoming aware of the existence of a European socio-economic model that seems to be characterised by high labour costs but also by high labour productivity, yielding high unemployment (and other forms of discarding from the labour market) that is taken care of by elaborate systems of social protection. Such an approach rests on an intensive interference of the state in society. The recent political rhetoric for more market, deregulation, consumer freedom, labour mobility and flexibility, and for the abolishment of minimum wage and income levels can hardly hide its plea for an American implantation in this European model. The US model rests indeed on less government intervention. It focuses on low labour costs but yields lower labour productivity and low unemployment rates but provides also a low level of social protection. Together with the low wages this limited degree of social protection generates a high poverty incidence and complex situations of social exclusion. (For some productivity indicators on the US and EU, see Table 5.)

So the question arises as to what extent Europe will be obliged, willing and politically capable of imputing American characteristics into its own model. This European model apparently encompasses mechanisms that induce high productivity and this is welcome in a time of global competition. On the other hand, however, there is some urge to adjust it given the high unemployment rate and the heavy social protection budget burden it yields and the trend towards dualisation of labour participation this engenders, with especially the lower skilled and less productive strata of the labour force as the categories that become at long-term risk.

Who negotiates the new social contract?

The broader labour-income nexus rests on a social contract that gets shaped through the policy struggle between the major socio-economic parties involved. Yet, it is becoming increasingly unclear which parties are involved, and to what extent their organisations and spokes(wo)men can voice their viewpoints. This is the case at the European level, but also at the national level. Especially in the continental (and

Table 5 Productivity indicators – % differences (EU = 100)

	US		EU
GDP/capita	130	>	100
GDP/employed person	108	>	100
Number of hours worked	144	>	100
GDP/hours worked	89	<	100
Remuneration/hour	101	=	100
Productivity/remuneration	87	<	100

Source: Cichon, M. (1997) 'Can Europe afford the future financing of the Welfare State?', in A. Bosco and M. Hutsebaut (eds), *Social Protection in Europe: Facing up to Changes and Challenges*. Brussels, ETUI, p. 82

Scandinavian) countries in which the core social policies used to stem from the social partners and in which these policies used to be based on a social contract between these partners and not between the nation-state and its citizens, policy making becomes blurred. To the extent that full employment has implicitly been given up, that the large numbers of unemployed, of insufficiently skilled and of (early) retired are no longer represented by the unions, they are looking for new spokesmen and organize themselves in categorical movements. Such a setting will complicate policy making and will make it even more difficult to elaborate the taut balance that is necessary for society, at both the national and European level, to survive in both an efficient and equitable way.

3 France: the social welfare system and recent reforms

Introduction

For several years, most European countries have tried to reform their social welfare system (SWS[1]) in order to contain expenditure, to alleviate indirect costs on employment, to redefine the conditions governing retirement and calculation of pensions, to contain the growth of health care costs, to reorganise income support for the unemployed, to reduce the financial deficit of the system, and to target expenditure on those who need it most (European Commission, 1995). In France, chronic economic recession is curbing revenues from the social welfare system while social spending is constantly growing. The result is an increasing yearly deficit in the social budget. Today, difficulties in welfare policies are more a financial problem than a legitimacy crisis of the system.

The fundamental features of the French social welfare system are described below, followed by a discussion of social exclusion problems, and recent reform proposals and debates.

The French social welfare system

The French social welfare system is the historical result of market and family failures to provide several social benefits, and the constant refusal of the French state to create a large public welfare institution (Castel, 1995, p. 245; Baldwin, 1990, p. 164). The French social welfare system is considered a Bismarckian one, a corporatist one according to Andersen (1990), or a selective model (Ploug and Kvist, 1996, p. 50). It is a very complex and fragmented system (Baldwin, 1990, p. 172), distinguishing between a large set of welfare trade groups (workers/executives (*cadres*), wage earners/self-employed people, etc.), and covering specific social risks, mainly retirement, health, family and unemployment. As all Bismarckian systems, the French one is made up of a large contributory domain, and a narrow non-contributory one comprising the social assistance sector for poor and/or excluded people.

The contributory sector of the French system can be described by several major features.

- The contributory sector is based upon a social insurance model which tends to be differentiated by occupational groups. Inside each group, a paritarian principle between employers and employees is the basis of management and funding. Furthermore, the original French system is based upon social security through full-time paid work contributions.

- Only contributors are the social insured; that 'socially insured' standing defines individuals' social rights. Consequently, entitlements principally derive from social insurance rather than citizenship or residence. Historically, the sector is focused on the welfare of the workers and their families. Entitlements are derived mainly from employment, and family members' benefits rely on entitlements of the breadwinner.

Denis Bouget, Centre d'Économie des Besoins Sociaux (CEBS), Nantes.

- Social insurance covers social risks. The basic principle is equality for everybody confronted with risk, non-discrimination between risk-classes, and within each group of insured persons (Lattès, 1996, p. 15). The social insurance system creates a horizontal solidarity among employees and their families.

- Benefits are income-related and usually proportioned according to earnings (pensions, unemployment benefits, daily sickness benefit). The proportionality between benefits and earnings results from the compensatory idea of the social welfare system within groups of employees or workers. There are two main exceptions: health-care reimbursements which depend on the level and the type of health-care consumption, and family benefits which depend on the number and age of children, and the structure of the family. For several years, most benefits have been frozen in real terms.

- Social insurance is compulsory for each employee (and, today, for retirees and the unemployed for health care insurance). This characteristic removes the adverse selection effect. A small portion is left to supplementary insurance (partly compulsory).

- Insurance premiums are paid by employers and employees. Wages and professional incomes are the contribution basis; today, we must include pensions and unemployment benefits for health-care insurance. Premiums are calculated

as a fixed proportion of the individual wage, with an upper limit, a ceiling; above it, the contribution rate is lower (Figure 1). In fact, several reforms have gradually done away with ceilings, and the regressive system of contributions is becoming more and more proportional (Dupuis, 1995, p. 51), but decreasing marginal rates for pensions still remain.

Figure 1 shows the level of total social contributions, related to the level of wage of an employee.

A Bismarckian model cannot work without the upholding of public assistance for poor and vulnerable groups (children, disabled, or elderly people), which is a non-contributory sector (Eardley *et al.*, 1996a).

Outside the social welfare system, France has a legal minimum wage (SMIG from 1950 to 1969, SMIC since 1970) for all firms in the country.

Finally, the French system is based upon a low public subsidy principle (assistance to the poor), and a high public regulation power, a governmental oversight of the contributory sector.

In France, social expenditure accounted for 30 per cent of GDP in 1995, and had remained constant for three years.

Old people's pensions make up 42.7 per cent of the social expenditure, and health-care expenses represent 33.2 per cent. During the 1980s, both shares remained more or less constant. The share of family expenditure has constantly decreased since 1950 (15 per cent in 1995). The unemployment benefits' share remained very low until 1970 (1–2 per cent) but it has gradually increased since then (7.2 per

31

Figure 1 Social contributions schedule of executives (*cadres*) in 1970 and 1997

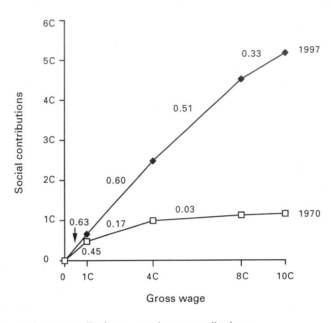

Notes
- Social contributions = employer contributions + employee contributions.
- Slopes represent marginal contribution rates.
- The income ceiling (*plafond de ressources*) is a threshold: 1C = FRF 13,720 in 1997; 4C = FRF 54,880. So, the social contributions unit on Figure 1 is defined as the ceiling in 1970 and 1997.
- Gross wage (French Social Security definition) = net wage + employee contributions.

Source: Dupuis (1994) and recent data.

cent in 1995). Three-quarters of social benefits are in cash benefits, instead of 80 per cent in 1960.

Until 1990, 75–80 per cent of the SWS revenues were paid for out of social insurance contributions, the highest share in Europe. This share has remained almost constant in the long term. Public authorities (central and local

Table 1 Social expenditure in 1995

	Social expenditure GDP (%)	Specific social expenditure/ total social expenditure (%)
Old age	12.7	42.7
Health	9.9	33.2
Family	4.6	15.3
Employment	2.1	7.2
Miscellaneous	0.5	1.6
Total	29.8	100

Source: SESI (1997), p. 36

authorities) financed only 20 per cent of the SWS revenues out of taxation. From the creation in 1991 of the generalised social contribution (*contribution sociale généralisée*, CSG) which is an income tax to help finance social security, and the progressive increase of the rate (1.1 per cent in 1991, up to 3.4 per cent in 1997), the share of public (tax-funded) contribution has increased. From 1950 to 1970, the contributory share between employers and employees has also remained constant (80 per cent/20 per cent). Since then, the employees' share has increased, including in the 1980s, up to 30 per cent today.

Social exclusion in France²

Until the 1970s, French society lived with a futurist ideology of a poverty-free society. But in the early 1980s, a 'new poverty' was described. Most roots of the increasing poverty for this decade originated in the economic field: unemployment, long-term unemployment, precariousness of the worker's condition (non-permanent work, low-paid process for young employees).

Social exclusion is a temporal process which hits several vulnerable groups: the unemployed, young people, wives, immigrants, etc. But, at the same time, we note several differences with past poverty. Firstly, in France, old people are not considered as a vulnerable group. In fact, the elderly and retirement policies since the 1960s can be deemed a success. Secondly, social exclusion is less a rural phenomenon than an urban problem. Thirdly, the temporal process of social exclusion creates a generational poverty: young people seem to be more and more vulnerable. Fourthly, a large part of poverty hits isolated people.

It is commonly acknowledged that France has 5 million poor, excluded people. In fact, it is very difficult to evaluate the number of poor people in France. There is not any official poverty line. The minimum income level, called the *revenu minimum d'insertion* (RMI) is often used as the reference for the poverty intensity measurement; in fact, the RMI is only one benefit among at least eight minimum incomes in France (Eardley, 1996a). At the end of 1995, almost one million people were entitled to RMI benefit and 1.6 million people were directly or indirectly its beneficiaries. If we add up all recipients of all kinds of minimum incomes, the frequency goes up to 3.3 million entitled recipients, and 6.6 million people who were directly or indirectly its beneficiaries; that is more than 11 per cent of the French population (Amrouni, Concialdi and Math, 1997).

Another evaluation of social exclusion in France is linked to exclusion from and precariousness within the labour market. At the end of 1995, 3.9 million employees were unemployed. Of these, 34.3 per cent were in long-term unemployment. But at the same time, we must take into account the recipients of all employment policy measures (1.5 million) and involuntary part-timers.

The OECD income study states that income inequality in France is in the middle range of European countries. More recent studies show that income inequality has not changed very much recently in France. However, several groups seem to be more vulnerable, especially young people: their unemployment ratio is very high and their wages are falling, relative to adult wages.

The terms in which social exclusion has been discussed have not changed in France for two

Table 2 Minimum incomes in France (per person)

	Monthly amount (FF) 1.1.97	Minimum income/ minimum wage (%)	Recipients 31.12.90	Recipients 31.12.95
SMIC (net minimum wage) (169 H/m)	5,038	100.0		
Allocation aux parents isolés (lone parent)	≥4,117	82.5	130,000	164,000
Minimum vieillesse (old people)	3,430	68.1	1,265	990,000
Minimum invalidité (disability)	3,430	68.1	132,000	105,000
Allocation aux adultes handicapés (disability)	3,430	68.1	527,000	616,000
Allocation veuvage (widowhood)	3,073 (first year) 2,019 (second year) 1,537 (after)	61.0	15,100	16,100
RMI	2,402	47.7	420,000	946,000 (993,900 on 30.6.96)
Allocation spécifique de solidarité (unemployment)	2,220	44.1	320,000	480,000
Allocation d'insertion (unemployment)	1,311	26.1	134,800	18,100

decades. The list of social reforms more or less linked to fighting against social exclusions is impressive, in several fields:

- *Employment policies*. The constant increase in unemployment in France (12.4 per cent in 1996), and the interpretation of long-term unemployment as the leading factor of social exclusion has put one part of employment policies more or less in the field of social exclusion policies: qualification training for unskilled workers and young people, several employers' social security contribution reliefs, etc; an act, called *la loi quinquennale relative au travail à l'emploi et à la formation professionnelle* (16 December 1993) has

tried to simplify and to plan the very complex and unstable employment policy in France, until 1998. Since the legislative elections (1 June 1997), the new government headed by the Socialists and L. Jospin, the Prime Minister, have decided to reform the previous act and to focus most new decisions on the employment of young people, and a reduction in working hours from 39 to 35 hours per week. The main aim of the government is to reduce the unemployment rate.

- *Urban and housing policies*. Urban policies began in the early 1980s with the *Développement social des quartiers* (DSQ), which progressively widened towards a more global cities policy (*politique de la ville*). In fact, the aim is always the same, to fight against all elements of disadvantage in areas of poverty. One of the new ideas is to create free zones in urban areas (*zones franches urbaines*), in which enterprises are partly free of taxes. This is an incentive to create new economic activity in disadvantaged urban areas. Housing is a fundamental right but the housing policy does not prevent people from being homeless.

- *Educational policies.* In this field, we note new policies against illiteracy.

- *Health policies.* See below.

- *Minimum incomes.* Since the creation of the *revenu minimum d'insertion* in France (1988), social exclusion has always been more or less on the political agenda.

Recent reforms of social protection

Most current drawbacks in the French model of social welfare regime arise from the need to achieve a universalist objective through the contributory system; elements of universalism and citizenship-based rights have been coupled to the dominant social insurance and contributory model. Despite the will of policy makers, it has always been impossible to bring together all categorial organisations in a unique body, a problem that all governments have to face. The paritarian rule fails to manage the SWS in a society which suffers from chronic unemployment; it cannot be an appropriate response to extensive social rights for all citizens

or residents. This evolution has led to an inconsistent situation between the small financial contribution of the state and its great juridical involvement. Governmental interventions have gradually become commonplace (allowance amounts, eligibility criteria, etc.), without any change in their financial contributions until the early 1990s.

The Juppé plan in 1995 and the bill on social cohesion in 1996-97 have been the most important events in the social protection field.

From Juppé to Jospin
In a speech on 15 November 1995 in the Chamber of Deputies, the Prime Minister, Alain Juppé, presented a plan to reform the social welfare system. The end of November and December 1995 were dominated by strikes. The immediate consequence was the withdrawal of the proposal on pensions in the public sector. Throughout 1996 and 1997, there has been intensive legislative activity. Two ordinances[3] have been promulgated on measures to clear the public debt. In February 1996, the Parliament (two Assemblies) amended the French Constitution to give it some new competences in the management of the social welfare system. In April 1996, three other ordinances were promulgated on the containment of health-care expenditure, on hospital organization, and on the new social security organization. In March 1997, a law created the retirement saving plan (*plan d'épargne retraite*). Several bills, on universal health-care insurance, on financing mechanisms of social security, on family policy, and on policies for fighting social exclusion, were still pending and under discussion in Spring 1997, when legislative elections unexpectedly brought the left to power under a

Socialist prime minister, Lionel Jospin.

The aim of the Juppé plan was threefold:

- to solve some of the financial drawbacks of the SWS
- to improve justice
- to avoid negative effects on employment.

The Juppé reform was mainly devoted to the health-care sector and the funding of social protection. As we shall see, the change of government has not caused a delay in the implementation of the Juppé plan.

The health-care system

The major topic in the Juppé plan was focused on health reform. The doctrinal principle was clearly expressed: 'In the name of justice we have decided on social security for all'. In the field of health, that means 'there is a right to the same benefits in kind for all'. This decision means a fundamental change in the social welfare system. Health care would become a citizenship-based right.

The plan proposed to create a universal health insurance regime. Rules for planning the financial support of health services would be reinforced. Parliament would have new responsibilities. Every year, it would have to decide objectives in health care at the national level, and to determine the expenditure trend and the revenues amount. New regional institutions (regional health-care agencies) were created for improving the planning of health care and for achieving several objectives: reduction of regional inequalities in the supply of care, quality evaluation of health-care activity (especially of hospitals), co-ordination between private and public hospitals, etc.

All these proposals have been implemented,

and the Jospin government has decided not to change this trend which results in an increasingly planned decision-making process.

The Juppé plan proposed a shift of the financing source from social insurance towards an income tax, especially a more intensive use of the generalized social contribution (CSG), created in 1991 by the Socialist Prime Minister, Michel Rocard. In 1996, the Juppé government increased the CSG rate up to 3.4 per cent. The Jospin government has decided to speed up the substitution of income tax for social contributions. The new proposal is to increase the CSG rate from 3.4 per cent up to 7.5 per cent and to reduce the employee contribution from 5.6 per cent to 0.75 per cent, in order to maintain purchasing power.

The supply structure of health care, in hospitals and ambulatory health care, is more and more under control. For two or three decades, whatever the government, a lot of health reforms have focused on financial control of activity in the health sector.

Pensions

In July 1993, the Balladur government reformed pension funding. In the private sector, pensions are now assessed on the basis of incomes over the best 25 wage years, instead of the best ten years. The period of contribution in working life must be 40 years instead of 37.5 years as before. All these reforms have been implemented to cut future benefits, but they remain in the same pay as you go (PAYG) system. The Juppé plan kept this system, without any increase in contribution rates. The Juppé government failed to extend the Balladur reform to the public sector and to specific occupational regimes (strikes). Jospin's government has not proposed any reform of pensions in the public sector.

The Juppé plan also proposed the possibility of saving for future private pensions. The creation of the retirement saving plan (*plan d'épargne retraite*) has been voted on by Parliament and it was promulgated in March 1997, after an appeal from left parties before the Constitutional Court. They considered the reform to be a liberal and conservative decision which could destroy the French pay as you go system. During the electoral campaign, Jospin promised the abolition of the act. Today, the implementation of the law seems to be halted.

Family benefits

In the name of equity, Juppé proposed a reorganization of the structure of benefits to make them simpler. In France, a proportion of family benefits is means-tested (45 per cent), another part is not, especially family allowances *allocations familiales*. Furthermore, there are several income threshold effects. The final result of that redistribution is not clear. In the name of equity, the Juppé plan proposed to target family benefits on those who are most in need, in fact on poor families. The plan also proposed to include family benefits in the income tax basis. A bill had to specify the content of these aims when … the government changed.

Of the Juppé proposals, Jospin has decided to change the *allocations familiales*, which were non-means-tested benefits, into a new means-tested allowance. In fact, this new vertical redistribution through the exclusion of rich families (more or less the upper decile), from the entitlement for the *allocations familiales*, has been decided mainly for the purpose of clearing the deficit of the social security system.

Funding mechanisms

In the Juppé plan, the reform of the funding of the social welfare system had three aims: to avoid a negative effect on the labour market, to reduce public deficit, and to obtain a consistency between general principles of the SWS and funding mechanisms.

The French system has to put a greater emphasis on tax-financed income transfers because more and more people have insufficient rights through the compulsory system for wage earners. The main proposals of the reform were:

- To widen the income CSG basis.

- In the health-care field to substitute gradually the CSG for social contributions. A bill will create a universal sickness insurance (*assurance maladie universelle*).

- To widen the employer's social security contribution basis to the added-value and not only on wages.

- To transfer responsibilities to Parliament which must decide on social expenditure, on its trend, and on the revenues for social protection.

- To create a social debt sinking fund (*caisse d'amortissement de la dette sociale*) which manages a new income tax named the social debt refund (*remboursement de la dette sociale*, RDS) in order to clear the debt of the social welfare system. The social debt will be reimbursed for a period of 13 years, by a tax rate of 0.5 per cent on a large tax basis.

All these proposals were implemented by the Juppé government before its dissolution, except the creation of the universal sickness insurance. Jospin's policies are likely to continue the implementation of Juppé's proposals. If the government decides to increase the CSG rate up to 7.5 per cent, the new amount of this proportional income tax will equal the progressive income tax (FRF 300 billion).

Fostering social cohesion

The failure of the French SWS can be considered a structural one because social institutions are unable to solve the increasing trend of social exclusion, in a society that wants greater cohesion. Excluded people are entitled to benefits as citizens, but receive only 'solidarity' benefits, in fact a public local or national assistance.

A bill for fostering social cohesion (*loi d'orientation relative au renforcement de la cohésion sociale*) was just under discussion in Parliament when it was dissolved for the election. Even if this bill is abandoned, the Jospin government is (politically) obliged to prepare a new one. So it is relevant to describe the previous bill.

The reform was an idea, a wish and more or less a proposal from the anti-poverty group (*ATD quart monde*), which firmly supported (with criticism) the governmental text. This bill tried to improve social cohesion in society, to refuse the polarisation process in most European countries (called the *fracture sociale* in France) and the split between the 'socially insured' status and the 'assisted' status. The bill recorded most daily elements of social exclusion, and proposed new practical solutions against barriers to access, or solutions to fulfil 'holes' in civil, political and social rights. The bill enunciated the principle that the fight against social exclusion is always on the agenda.

The bill tried to improve fundamental conditions of access to social rights (basic rights, equality of opportunities): citizenship (homeless, families, immigrants, non-French nationals), employment (young unemployed, a new measure (*contrat d'initiative locale*) for long-term unemployed), housing (requisitioning empty homes, water, electricity, creation of new public housing, homelessness), health (guarantee of access to health services), culture (policy against illiteracy). A local initiative contract (*contrat d'initiative locale*) was to turn passive benefits (RMI) into active benefits (wages), by granting employment in the local public sector.

The bill tried also to harmonize involved institutions. The *département* (both administrative and political powers located between the region and the municipality area) was recognized as the leading institutional tier for fighting social exclusion. This responsibility was implemented through a local plan. Among institutions providing social services, shelter centres (*centre d'hébergement et de réhabilitation sociale*) were reformed. The bill planned also an improvement of social workers' training. The bill included an action programme (*programme d'action*).

So the reform was mainly bent on improving the efficiency of current institutions, rules, information, etc. However, while everybody accepted the need to enhance the fight against social exclusion through an improvement of the labour market and an easier access to social rights, several consultative assemblies severely criticized the project. For instance, it hardly simplified the set of minimum incomes. The bill did not propose any new important benefit, or any income tax reform. The social cohesion reform had no substantial new funding mechanism, nor any deep change in social institutions. The leading criticism was that the bill did not clearly show a political goal of global social cohesion in the whole society, but only a rearrangement of social cohesion among poor and excluded people, by cutting some entitlements, to fund others: the poor paid for the poorest.

Today, Jospin's government has to propose a project which will be partly a response to criticisms of the previous one.

Conclusion

Policies for fighting poverty are becoming more and more complex because of the embeddedness of social institutions. The present intervention of public authorities may be seen as a set of social policies which are trying to compensate for the failure of the contributory system.

At the same time, all governments have to solve the problem of the chronic financial deficit of the SWS. Maastricht criteria are very often blamed for fuelling not only an economic recession but also a dismantling of social protection in France. The paradox today is that several decisions which are taken in the name of equity (health services, poor families) are in fact mainly implemented in order to obey the Maastricht criteria.

References

Amrouni, I., Concialdi, P. and Math, A. (1997) *Les Minima Sociaux, 25 Ans de Transformation*, Les dossiers de CERC-association, No. 2

Andersen, E. (1990) *The Three Worlds of Welfare Capitalism*. Polity Press

Baldwin, P. (1990) *The Politics of Social Solidarity, Class Bases of the European Welfare State 1875–1975*. Cambridge: Cambridge University Press, pp. 353

Bouget, D. (1996) 'The French social welfare system and the Juppé plan', Working Paper Series, No. 3. Copenhagen: Center for Welfare State Research

Bouget, D. and Dupuis, J.M. (1997) 'Les politiques sociales' in R. Duthil and W. Marois (eds) *Politiques Économiques*. Ellipses

Castel, R. (1995) *Les Métamorphoses de la Question Sociale, Chronique du Salariat*. Fayard

Commission of the European Communities (1994) *Europe, Social Protection in 1993*. Brussels: Directorate General V

Conseil Économique et Social (1995) 'Évaluation des politiques publiques de lutte contre la grande pauvreté, avis et rapports du CES', *Journal Officiel*, No. 3, July

Dupeyroux, J.J. (1995) *Droit de la Sécurité Sociale*. Dalloz.

Dupeyroux, J.J. (1996) 'Le plan Juppé: introduction', *Droit Social*, No. 3, March, pp. 13–20

Dupuis, J.M. (1994) *Le Financement de la Protection Sociale*. Presses Universitaires de France, pp. 128

Eardley, T., Bradshaw, J., Ditch, J., Gough, I. (1996a) *Social Assistance in OECD Countries: Synthesis Report*, Research Report No. 46. OECD-HMSO, Department of Social Security

Eardley, T., Bradshaw, J., Ditch, J., Gough, I. (1996b) *Social Assistance in OECD Countries: Synthesis Report*, Research Report No. 47. OECD-HMSO, Department of Social Security

European Commission (1995) *Europe, Social Protection in 1995*. Brussels: Directorate General V

Guibentif, P. and Bouget, D. (1997) *Minimum Income Policies in the European Union*. Lisbon: Uniao Das Mutualidades

Lattès, G. (1996) 'La protection sociale: entre partage des risques et partage des revenus', Insee, *Economie et Statistique*, No. 291–292, pp. 13–32

Paier, B. (1997) 'A liberal dynamic in the transformation of the French social welfare', in J. Classen (ed.) *Social Insurance in Europe*. Bristol: Policy Press, pp. 84–106

Ploug, N. and Kvist, J. (1996) 'Social security in Europe, development or dismantlement?', *Kluwer Law International, Kluwer Socac Series on Social Security*, Vol. 3

Prate, A. (1996) 'L'endettement public, avis et rapports du Conseil Économique et Social', *Journal Officiel*, No. 11, March

Robbins, D. (ed.) (1994) *National Policies to Combat Social Exclusion, Third Annual Report*. Observatory on National Policies to Combat Social Eclusion, CCE-DGV

Room, D. (ed.) (1991), *National Policies to Combat Social Exclusion, First Annual Report*. Observatory on National Policies to Combat Social Eclusion, CCE-DGV

SESI (1997) *Les Comptes de la Protection Sociale 1990-1995*. Ministère du Travail et des Affaires Sociales

Zaïdman, C. (1996), 'Le régime universel: les objectifs et les difficultés de sa mise en place', *Droit Social*, No. 3, March, pp. 333–8

Notes

1   *Système de protection sociale*, in France.

2   For a more detailed description of social assistance institutions in France, see Eardley T. *et al*. (1996b), p. 143.

3   A constitutional procedure which gives the government the legal right to create juridical texts which are considered laws. In 1945, the social security organization was created by the same procedure (ordinance on 4 October 1945).

4 The German welfare state: status quo and perspectives

Introduction

The Member States of the European Union, which differ from each other in many ways including their 'welfare stateness', are nevertheless characterised by common elements that contribute in varying 'mixes' to their respective welfare systems. These elements include:

- *Democracy*: a constitutional system based on democratic foundations.

- *The market economy*: a market-oriented economic system in which the state nevertheless intervenes to 'correct' in various ways.

- *Social protection*: a well-developed system for preventing social risks and, where they materialise, taking compensatory action. At the same time each system maintains private obligations and relies within households on informal services, performed mainly by women, to complete the system of social welfare.

- *Inclusion*: a broad field of socio-political activities aimed at reducing discrimination and inequality of opportunity, creating possibilities for personal development and – in general – at integrating members of society into its activities.

- *The rule of law*: a legal system guaranteeing the possibility for citizens to participate in social measures and benefits on the basis of law, especially in the form of individual legal entitlements.

Bernd Schulte, Max Planck Institute, Munich.

A welfare state of this kind can be termed a social state, in which the above elements constitute a *normative* obligation laid down on the state by law and especially by the constitution. Germany in this sense considers itself a social state (*Sozialstaat*) because the social aim of the state is entrenched in the constitution or basic law, and is intrinsically linked to the fundamental state principles of democracy, the republic, federalism and the rule of law (Articles 20 and 28GG).

After the Second World War, against the background of the new basic law, the concept of a 'social market economy' (*Soziale Marktwirtschaft*) was conceived and realised. This concept combines elements of a free market economy with strong labour market regulations, worker co-determination, and a social security system which is, by tradition, based on the social *insurance* principle that maintains the living standards of the insured regardless of 'social risks' – sickness, maternity, invalidity, accidents at work, occupational disease, old age and unemployment. In addition, a minimum of subsistence is guaranteed via social *assistance* and measures to alleviate the economic burden on families are provided. The system was created in the 1950s as a result of broad political consensus between the main political parties and the 'social partners' – trade unions and employers' associations.

Main features of German social protection

Social protection in Germany is provided largely through the insurance principle, with social assistance providing an additional safety net.

Employees and most categories of the self-employed are insured against the risk of loss of income in the event of sickness, maternity, invalidity, occupational accident and disease, old age, death of the breadwinner and unemployment. The contribution and cash-benefit levels aim at income replacement proportional to wage income. Housewives and children are to a large extent covered indirectly as dependants of the insured earner. Voluntary insurance of those who are not compulsorily covered by social insurance schemes is possible.

In addition to the means-tested social assistance scheme, which provides a general safety net for those inadequately insured, family benefits, housing allowances and educational allowances provide social benefits to meet more specific needs.

This system has been operated on the basis of a number of strong principles.

The centrality of contributory insurance
In the German system, a strong link is preserved between contribution and benefit levels, both of which are roughly proportional to wage income, although in both cases there are upper and lower limits, so that low wage-earners for example receive special protection. This simple principle is designed to ensure that social protection is compatible with a free, achievement-oriented society. It is also deemed to support the principle of subsidiarity, in that private individuals provide as far as possible for their own social security. Unlike the case of means-tested social assistance, the insurance principle involves a legal entitlement to benefits subject to no other condition than that

contributions have previously been paid. Contributory funds are strictly earmarked and cannot by law be touched by the State and diverted to other purposes.

Because of the directness of the link between contributions and benefits, a high level of contributions has been sustained without being regarded as unduly punitive taxation. This has made possible a generous level of benefits. In the case of the old age pension, for example, the rates are not only linked directly to former wage levels, but indeed are in line with net wages. The present rate is 64 per cent for those who retire at the normal age.

However, while relatively high contributions have been acceptable because, under stable conditions, workers know that they can expect to reap an equivalent benefit, this system can become more problematic under less stable conditions. Under Germany's 'pay as you go' system, today's workers face contributions that are high relative to their own expected benefits, for two reasons. First, because the size of the working-age population relative to the retired population is falling rapidly. Second, because the benefits of claimants from the Eastern part of Germany are effectively being subsidised by the contributions of those who live in the West. The growing cost of the system and the implications of reunification are discussed further below.

Division into separate branches
The division of the overall system of social insurance into five separate branches underlies its organisation. These branches are:

- sickness
- social care

- invalidity and old age
- accident and occupational disease
- unemployment.

Such subdivision allows tasks and responsibilities to be clearly defined. Since contribution rates are calculated for each branch, it also makes highly visible the purpose to which contributions are put.

The division into branches also allows for diversity of suppliers of social security, with employees who work full-time on average wages over a full working life being given some choice of providers. In the case of invalidity, old age and invalidity pensions, for example, there is a so-called 'three pillar' principle, with statutory, occupational and private provision co-existing. The statutory scheme is designed to provide conventional income security, with the other types of provision playing a supplementary role. In the case of sickness insurance, on the other hand, there is competition within the statutory system itself: self-employed people, civil servants and high wage employees have the option of arranging alternative cover through private health insurance.

Administrative autonomy of the social insurance institutions

Those who are directly involved in the social insurance system run it themselves, without state interference. The co-operation of employers and employees on the one hand, and of service providers on the other, is used to steer the social insurance institutions. Administrative autonomy through decentralisation, deconcentration and deregulation helps both to enhance efficiency and gain the confidence of public opinion. The state is expected to restrict its role to the creation of the legal framework under which the system operates. This includes the establishment of self-governing bodies, which are subject only to legal supervision by the state.

Solidarity – that is, risk sharing among wage-earners

All social insurance is not risk-related but based on the principle of solidarity in the sense that there is a sharing of risks among the insured. In the field of social insurance, solidarity additionally means that contributions should rise in line with the income of the insured, and in statutory health and care insurance that spouses without income from work of their own, along with children, should be covered without additional contributions. In other words, social insurance implies a cross-subsidy from lower- to higher-risk workers and from those without dependants to those with dependants, but does not automatically imply subsidy from rich to poor or from those households included in the labour market to those who are excluded over long periods.

Pressures and change

The German system of social protection was continuously extended after the Second World War, with respect to whom it covered, what contingencies it provided for and the level of benefits. The first attempt to put a lid on this growth was introduced in the 1970s following the 'oil price shock': a Social Democrat-led government reduced benefits, tightened entitlement rules and changed the indexation formulas. But such economies were at the margin, and did not prevent the combined employer and employee contribution rate from rising progressively from 26.5 per cent in 1970 to 32.4 per cent in 1980 and 38.9 per cent in 1994. But this has not prevented the system from renewing itself to cater for fresh needs. In 1994 a whole new branch of social insurance was introduced, to provide for long-term care.

The introduction of long-term care insurance, the response to reunification and the reform of social assistance all illustrate ways in which the system is adapting to a new social and economic context.

Long-term care insurance

Long-term care insurance was developed in the mid-1990s as a separate, fifth branch of the social insurance system. The scheme is financed through contributions, which are shared equally between employers and employees, as is the case with other branches. Benefits are provided by the long-term care insurance funds, which are administered independently and whose duties are performed by the sickness funds in return for an administrative fee.

The need for long-term care is subdivided into three categories or nursing levels, according to people's needs – classed as 'considerable', 'severe' and 'extreme' need for care. The provision of benefits is governed by two principles: that prevention and rehabilitation come before nursing, and that home care is preferred to residential.

Where possible, the aim is to continue to maintain a traditional pattern of care within the family, and benefits are designed only to supplement family contributions and ease the financial burden of institutional care, rather than to transfer responsibility away from the family. One way in which this principle is

strengthened is by providing the option of substituting cash benefits for benefits in kind – allowing family members to do caring that might otherwise have been done by professionals, and to receive compensation for doing so.

This policy of encouraging family care is reflected in the old age and invalidity pension law, which gives contribution credits towards pension to people who take time out of paid work to care for children or dependants. The contribution credits are at the same rate as if they had been working. This extension of the pension scheme to activities other than remunerative work is a significant move towards tackling the challenge of the changing nature of work and its impact on the system of social protection.

The provision of long-term care itself is primarily left to voluntary welfare organisations, in line with the principle of subsidiarity mentioned above. These non-profit organisations are traditionally linked to religious and ideological foundations, including the labour movement. In view of the long tradition of social insurance in Germany, which goes back to the 1880s, it is not surprising that the need for long-term care was tackled in this way rather than through the market.

In introducing this new benefit, however, some regard had to be given to the growing concern about the overall burden of social insurance, especially to employers. The total cost was equivalent to 1.7 per cent of the wage bill, of which employers were expected to contribute one-half. At first, they wanted to break with the equal contribution principle, and asked the entire contribution to be made by labour. This was not acceptable to labour representatives, who nevertheless recognised the potential damage to competitiveness that could arise from yet another social charge. As a compromise, the employers continue to make equal contributions, but the unions agreed to increase working time by a day a year to help compensate, by removing one public holiday.

Reunification and the affordability of the social state

German reunification in 1989 imposed an additional large burden on the German welfare state. The social expenditure of West Germany was 30.4 per cent of its GDP in 1989; for unified Germany in 1993 the figure was 34 per cent. This increase resulted mainly from high transfers via the social insurance system from West to East. The treaty of union provided for a transfer of the West German social protection system to the East, albeit at benefit levels based on East German wages, which, however, rose faster than productivity in the years following reunification. East German beneficiaries who have made relatively low contributions, but whose relatively lengthy contribution records boost their entitlements, are now getting high benefit incomes relative to what they have put in. At the same time, high unemployment in the East and a declining yield due to demographic and economic factors require higher contributions that hit West Germans hard.

While the transformation of the East German system of social protection led to big increases in most of the earnings-related benefits, especially pensions (East German pensioners considerably improving their income relative to both wage earners and West German pensioners), there was a sharp decline in the provision of social services that had formerly been provided by the state and state-run enterprises now transformed into 'market economy style' firms which had shed their social tasks. Meanwhile, unemployment has grown to the highest level since the Second World War – 4.7 million at the beginning of 1997.

The social state has been criticised in recent years as never before since its creation. *Laissez-faire* liberals argue that the high labour costs in Germany are the main causes of the high rate of unemployment. Supporters of the traditional, work-oriented social state defend their vested interests and oppose any reduction in rights and entitlements. This debate has recently been heightened by the Maastricht convergence criteria. Recent economies have included:

- A restructuring of health provision to increase patients' contributions to the cost of hospital stays and a cash limit on spending by statutory health insurance funds to ensure that it is covered by contributions.

- The introduction of new measures to help integrate unemployed people into work, not as previously paid for by the insurance scheme but mainly funded by the federal government, which also offers subsidies to employers of people who would otherwise be jobless.

- Cuts to the level of replacement income payments, including unemployment benefit, short-time allowances, bad weather money and integration allowances, by 1–3 per cent.

Reform of social assistance

In 1995 there were 2.5 million recipients of social assistance. The number of beneficiaries had risen by about 8 per cent over the previous year. A reform of social assistance in 1996 aimed to make this 'safety net' more efficient, and emphasised both the prevention of poverty and integration into the labour market. The poor are now mainly the young, the long-term unemployed, large families and one-parent families. In this context, recent social assistance legislation has tended to link income replacement with obligation and opportunity to work. There is also an attempt to make social assistance more efficient by better targeting and prevention of fraud.

The unemployment rate is still the most important social issue in Germany and will remain so for some years. As demonstrated by the growing number of homeless people, the provision of adequate housing is also an important social issue, because of the rise in single-person households – now 50 per cent in big cities – and migration to urban areas and changing lifestyles.

5 Income protection, inclusion and exclusion in Ireland

An overview of the system and present trends

The Irish system of income protection can be characterised by three key features:

- Contributory or social insurance payments made on the basis of Pay Related Social Insurance (PRSI) contributions in the event of certain contingencies (for example, illness, unemployment). They are funded by employers' and workers' contributions, and the Exchequer.

- Non-contributory or social assistance payments are made on the basis of claimants satisfying a means test and are totally Exchequer funded.

- Universal payments such as Child Benefit and Free Travel do not depend on either PRSI contributions or means tests.

Both contributory and non-contributory payments cover pensions, unemployment and long-term invalidity and disablement. In addition, there are social assistance payments for carers and lone parents. Payments consist of a personal rate and additional amounts for adult and child dependants.

Supplementary Welfare Allowance (SWA) is a safety-net scheme for those not in work and it guarantees a minimum income (£62.40 in 1996/ 97) to those who are neither eligible for social insurance nor covered by the contingency-based social assistance schemes. The SWA also provides supplementary and exceptional needs payments for those in receipt of regular payments from it and other schemes.

Retirement

Over the period 1973–87 the position of the elderly with regard to poverty improved considerably. This was mainly the result of significant increases in the real value of social welfare old age pensions. However, in the late 1980s and early 1990s, support rates for the elderly rose by a good deal less than mean incomes. As a result, by 1994 (date of the most recent national survey information available) many of those relying on old age pensions were on incomes of about half average household income, whereas in 1987 (the date of the previous survey) they had been comfortably above half average income. This was the result of giving priority to increasing the lowest rates of social welfare payments.

Of the 415,000 people in the state over age 65, about 325,000 are recipients of state pensions. They have about 52,000 dependants. Coverage is over 90 per cent overall. The total expenditure in 1996 on weekly pensions and cash allowances to those aged 65 or over amounted to IR£1,300m, an average of £77 per week per recipient.

Disability

In 1995, 85,000 adults who had disabilities were in receipt of a state payment. This included 42,000 people on Invalidity Pension, some of whom may have had other sources of income. However, the 33,000 people on Disabled Persons Maintenance Allowance (DPMA), a means-

Helen Johnston, Head of Research, and Hugh Frazer, Director, Combat Poverty Agency, Dublin.

tested benefit, are unlikely to have other sources of income, and thus are dependent on state support.

People with disabilties were identified in 1994 as having a high risk of poverty, having increased substantially since 1987. A recent report produced by a Commission on the Status of People with Disabilities (1996) has noted that many people with disabilities live close to the poverty line, because they are prevented from working and/or on account of the additional costs associated with disability. There are a bewildering array of schemes, matched by an equally bewildering set of eligibility and assessment procedures.

Unemployment

Unemployment Benefit rates of payment are still below lowest minimally adequate rate recommended by a Commission on Social Welfare (CSW) which reported in 1986 – £50 per week for a single person in 1985 terms, equivalent to £68.10 in 1996 terms. From June 1996 Unemployment Benefit (contributory payment) is £64.50 or 95 per cent of this CSW rate. The highest rates of Unemployment Assistance (means-tested payment) are also below the CSW rate, at £64.50. Various government programmes have been committed to working towards this minimally adequate rate and there have been significant improvements in the lowest payments in recent years, thus contributing to a reduction in the depth of poverty. However, the unemployed, particularly unemployed heads of households, make up the biggest proportion of those living in poverty and people who are unemployed have a high risk of poverty, especially larger families. This is scarcely surprising given the persistently high levels of unemployment and especially of long-term unemployment. While recently there has been a downward trend in unemployment from 18 per cent in 1987 the overall level is still high. More importantly high levels of long-term unemployment have persisted and the long-term unemployed have not gained from the very high levels of job creation in the Irish economy.

Unemployment Benefit is of fixed duration. In Ireland entitlement ceases after 15 months, with those who remain unemployed moving to Unemployment Assistance, subject to a means test. Increasingly, however, unemployment is no longer a temporary phenomenon. About half of the 280,000 people registered as unemployed at the beginning of 1996 had been unemployed for one year or more. Fewer than one-quarter of the unemployed are paid an insurance benefit. This is either because they have exhausted their entitlement to benefit after 15 months or because they were unable to build up an entitlement to benefit in the first instance.

Families with children

Every mother in the country gets a flat-rate, tax-free Child Benefit payment for each child. There are higher payments for third-plus children. The amount of Child Benefit, even though it has been substantially increased in recent years, remains small (£6.70/£7.85 per week, 1996) compared to the overall costs associated with rearing a child (estimated at £34.50 per week in 1996). Unemployed parents and lone parents receive £13.20/£15.20 per week per child in addition to Child Benefit.

In 1995, 354,000 children were living in families receiving the full-rate child dependent allowance (mainly where either both parents were unemployed or where the family was headed by a single parent). This amounts to about one-third of the state's children who are dependent on the state for their upbringing. The level of child poverty in Ireland is high with a 29 per cent poverty risk for children at half average income compared to a 18 per cent risk for adults. This has increased from 26 per cent in 1987. Unemployment has been identified as the main reason for the high level of child poverty in Ireland.

There has been a substantial growth in the number of one-parent families in Ireland. The majority of lone parents are dependent on the state for their main source of income. Recent studies have shown their incomes to be below minimally adequate rates and in 1994 lone parents were one of the groups at greatest risk of poverty. However, in recent years payment rates have increased, earnings disregards have improved significantly and treatment in relation, and participation on community employment schemes has increased.

Housing costs

At present, a wide range of direct and indirect subsidies towards housing costs is provided through the social welfare system, through various tax reliefs and through local authorities, as well as a number of smaller schemes. The existence of a number of schemes results in gaps in overall provision, as well as inconsistencies in treatment. A particular problem is that some schemes, such as rent supplements (private rented) and mortgage supplements (owner occupied) and payment of differential rents (local authority housing) contribute to poverty and unemployment traps.

Table 1 shows that there have been substantial increases in the cost of social welfare benefits across the four categories. This is a result of a combination of an increased number of recipients and a higher level of payment for some of the main benefits. However, there has been a large increase in the number of people receiving means-tested (social assistance) payments – increasing from 320,000 in 1986 to 434,000 in 1996.

Table 1 Real spending on social security payments to four groups: 1971–96

	1981*	1986	1991	1996†
		IR£000		
Old age	293,101	719,096	903,358	
Illness	131,361	356,205	363,831	
Family Income Support	186,317	590,515	810,958	
Unemployed	189,969	665,008	840,657	
Total	**800,748**	**2,330,824**	**2,918,804**	
Social Assistance Payments				
(SAPs) – (means tests)	311,159	1,106,575	1,186,031	
SAPs as % total	39	47	41	

Notes:
* excludes free schemes.
† full data for 1996 not available at time of going to press.

Underlying trends and income exclusion

Trends in poverty and social exclusion

- In 1994 about one-fifth of the population fell below half average household income – often cited as the 'poverty line' (about £65 for a single adult).

- There was an increase of about 2 per cent in the numbers experiencing poverty since 1987.

- While the numbers experiencing poverty increased, the depth of their poverty had been reduced, that is, their incomes did not fall as far below the poverty line as they did in 1987.

- When income poverty is combined with non-monetary deprivation indicators, for example, not having a warm winter coat or a substantial meal in the day, the overall number of people experiencing poverty is lower – between 9 per cent and 15 per cent of the population – these people are considered to be experiencing long-term poverty and are consistently poor.

- There has been about a 1 per cent reduction in the consistently poor since 1987.

- Households headed by an unemployed person were the largest group in poverty in 1994, representing about one-third of all households in poverty, with households headed by someone working full-time in the home making up the next largest group of households in poverty.

- The groups at greatest risk of poverty are: the unemployed, particularly the long-term unemployed; children, particularly those living in large families; heads of household, particularly older women living alone; lone parents; people with disabilities; travellers; and people out of home.

- Other less easily identifiable groups may also be at risk, particularly through discrimination, but evidence on their levels of poverty is difficult to obtain.

Demographic trends

The current demographic position in Ireland is more favourable now than at any other time in Ireland's recent history. Ireland remains unique in EU terms, in that over the next 20 years any 'greying' of the population will be counterbalanced by reduced child dependency and increasing female labour force participation. In fact, Ireland will have fewer dependants per worker in the future than there have been in the recent past. These lower economic dependency levels will lessen demands on the welfare state and free up resources.

Economic and social trends

Ireland is experiencing exceptional rates of growth which are being translated into high levels of job creation and rising living standards. However, this economic growth has not eradicated unemployment, particularly long-term unemployment and poverty, and social inequalities have widened in recent decades.

Adequacy of benefit levels

There are differing views on the adequacy of social welfare payments. A recent research study which reviewed rates of minimum adequate income stated that there is no one unproblematic, objective and scientific method which allows the derivation of income adequacy estimates which would be universally acceptable and convincing. The researchers argued that statements about adequacy reflect judgements, values and attitudes and that research cannot substitute for, but can inform, such judgements. Nevertheless, the current national government programme is committed to achieving a minimally adequate rate set by a Commission on Social Welfare in 1986 – which is £68.10 in 1996 terms. The recent research study referred to above arrived at a range of rates from £68 to £96 depending on the methodology employed. The current challenge is to arrive at a rate which is adequate and will prevent poverty but will not unduly affect work incentives. A recent Working Group to the National Anti-Poverty Strategy stated that:

All policies in relation to income support – whether these policies relate to employment, tax, social welfare, occupational pensions or otherwise should aim to provide sufficient income for all those concerned to move out of poverty and to live in a manner compatible with human dignity.

Policy trends and debates

Pensions

The Department of Social Welfare has recently published a consultation document on a national pensions policy initiative. The purpose of the document is to stimulate the public debate on the national pensions system leading to recommendations on the future shape of national pensions policy. A recent research study has found that over 50 per cent of workers in Ireland are not covered for occupational pensions. In considering the future overall pension policy for Ireland the consultation document states that the objective must be to achieve 100 per cent occupational coverage for people, ensuring a reasonable standard of living on retirement. Ireland is in the fortunate position of having time to devise a

Table 2 Key facts 1996

Value of	IR£ per week	As % of average disposable household income (£292)*	As % of average income per adult equivalent (£135)*
Old age non-contributory (state) pension	£64.50	22	48
Old age contributory pension	£75.00	26	55
Unemployment Benefit	£64.50	22	48
Family with two young children on Unemployment Assistance	£141.86	49	105
Basic payment (SWA) for a single person	£62.40	21	46

Note: * uprated for inflation from figures derived from 1994 *Living in Ireland* survey. (The average level of the CPI rose by 2.5 per cent in 1995 and 1.75 per cent in 1996.)

comprehensive pensions policy in that it is not facing a 'pensions time-bomb', unlike its European neighbours.

Means tests versus contingent benefits

In Ireland spending on social insurance (contingency) and social assistance (means-tested) weekly payments are similar in size, but the mix of income support contingencies met by social insurance is different to that met by social assistance. About two-thirds of social insurance recipients are pensioners and one-sixth are unemployed people. In contrast, almost one-half of social assistance recipients are unemployed people while only one-third are pensioners. The growth in unemployment, particularly long-term unemployment has been the most influential factor affecting the social insurance/ assistance balance. The government has recently published a discussion document on the future of social insurance in Ireland, setting out a number of potential policy options.

In-work benefits

Family Income Supplement (FIS) is a weekly cash payment available to help families on low pay who are working for at least 19 hours per week. In 1995 there were 11,400 families in receipt of FIS. There are two key difficulties with FIS: these are the contribution of the withdrawal rate to the poverty trap and the low take-up of the benefit by those entitled to it. There is a government commitment to calculate FIS on a net income basis rather than on gross wages, as is the case currently.

'Welfare to work'

There has been an increasing emphasis on assisting people to move from welfare to work.

This has resulted in a number of schemes initiated specifically for this purpose, for example, the Back to Work Allowance, as well as a number of initiatives to help people make the transition, for example, retention of secondary benefits for a period. In June 1996 an Expert Working Group produced a report on *Integrating Tax and Social Welfare* with an emphasis on facilitating the move from welfare to work. This group examined a range of issues and made a number of strategic recommendations in relation to reducing tax on the lower paid through increasing tax allowances and through improving child income support. The group also examined the potential of a basic income approach but did not recommend this option.

Families

In 1995 the government set up a Commission on the Family to examine the needs and priorities of families in a rapidly changing social and economic environment. The Commission was due to report by June 1997. Ireland has traditionally held very conservative family values – however, while the Commission has to have due regard to the provisions on the family as set out in the Irish Constitution (which is intended to support the family unit), it has also to reflect the definition of the family as described by the UN – that is, that the family is a basic unit of society in all its forms, whether traditional, biological, common law, extended or one parent.

National anti-poverty strategy

For the past two years the Irish government has been drawing up a national anti-poverty strategy (NAPS). The NAPS is a major cross-departmental policy initiative by the government designed to place the needs of people living in poverty and socially excluded at the top of the national agenda in terms of policy development and action. In essence it represents an effort to mainstream anti-poverty action and learning pioneered by the Combat Poverty Agency and others in recent years. The development of the NAPS has involved wide-ranging consultation and participation with the voluntary and community sector, the Social Partners, academics and researchers, users of services and those with first-hand experience of poverty. In developing the NAPS a number of key theme areas have been identified, and targets and action programmes have been developed around them. These are long-term unemployment, educational disadvantage, income adequacy, concentrations of urban disadvantage and rural poverty. A particularly important aspect of NAPS has been the identification of a number of institutional arrangements to ensure that poverty is, and remains, at the heart of the policy-making process and cuts across the whole range of departments and agencies. Also provisions are being put in place to ensure ongoing monitoring and evaluation of the strategy and public and institutional awareness raising in relation to the strategy. The NAPS was due to be published and launched by the Government on 23 April 1997.

The importance of the NAPS is reinforced by the agreement of a new national development plan, *Partnership 2000*, between the government, the Social Partners and the community and voluntary sector. This sets out national priorities for the next three years and includes a basic deal on wage increases and taxation. Within this

programme the issue of poverty and social exclusion is given a very high priority and specific reference in made to NAPS.

One of the key issues that has arisen during the preparation of NAPS has been the link between national policy making and local action in addressing issues of poverty and social exclusion. A very important policy initiative has been the development of a national local development programme targeted on 38 of the most disadvantaged urban and rural communities. This has raised questions as to what extent social inclusion can be addressed through local action and how can national policies, including social welfare policies, reinforce local action to promote social inclusion. Interestingly the stuctures that have been developed at local level involve partnerships between statutory agencies, the traditional Social Partners and local communities, and mirror the adoption of a partnership and the growth of social corporatism at a national level.

What lies ahead?

Ireland is at a cross-roads. On the one hand the combination of very favourable economic trends coupled with a significant demographic dividend means there could be significant resource buoyancy for addressing issues of poverty and social exclusion. On the other hand there is the danger that rapid economic and technological changes and the globalisation of the world economy, coupled with changes in family and social structures, could lead to an increasingly polarised or dual society. In essence the project that Ireland is currently engaging in with the National Anti-Poverty Strategy,

Partnership 2000, and the focus on local development is to reconcile continued economic and social change, and progress with promoting social integration and inclusion.

At the core of the emerging Irish model of develoment lie three core understandings. First, that poverty and social exclusion are deep-seated structural problems which will not be solved merely by the benefits of economic growth trickling down. Second, the causes of poverty and social exclusion are multi-dimensional and will not be solved by income measures alone. Third, that if a more inclusive society is to be developed it will need a strategic approach and will require the development of a national consensus in favour of a more integrated society. This will need to be underpinned by the fostering of partnership at both national and local levels between government, the traditional Social Partners and the voluntary and community sector.

While from the perspective of tackling poverty and social exclusion there are a number of favourable developments, the core debate over the next few years will continue to be who should benefit from the projected resource buoyancy. There is no basis for complacency as to the outcome of this debate. However, its outcome will be crucial in determining what can be done to promote social inclusion.

Whatever happens in the overall national debate about the allocation of resources, there are a number of specific policy debates that seem likely to be dominant over the next few years and will impact significantly on the future of social protection. At the broadest level there is the question of how the 'social inclusion cake' should be divided. That is, to what extent should it focus on providing immediate assistance through income support measures? Or should a higher priority be given to addressing some of the underlying causes of poverty and social exclusion such as educational disadvantage, poor access to public services, difficulties in accessing the labour market and spatial concentrations of poverty? More specifically there are a number of crucial issues and debates that appear to be emerging. For instance:

- Should there be more conditionality attached to the entitlement to social welfare payments?

- How can social welfare be developed as a stepping stone back into the labour force and how can it take account of increasing atypical, part-time and insecure work, and related to this how can there be greater integration between tax and social welfare systems to avoid disincentives to taking up work?

- What mechanisms should be put in place to link social welfare levels to rapidly increasing wages?

- What priority should be given to particular groups in society who are at risk of poverty, such as the elderly, the unemployed, lone parents, people with a disability, travellers? (At times this debate verges on a discussion of the 'deserving' and 'undeserving' poor.)

- How best can issues of child and family poverty be addressed, and in particular what are the best forms of child income support and how do you ensure equity between lone parent families and other families?

- Should some system of 'social guarantee' (for example, job, training, further education) be put in place so that no young person under a specified age (for example, 21) needs to avail of social protection and, if so, on what basis, compulsory or voluntary?

- What priority should be given to issues of gender and individualisation of payments *vis-à-vis* issues of poverty and social exclusion?

Finally, there is an underlying policy debate that has not been very clearly articulated up to now but which may well come more to the fore over the next period. If one's priority concern is to address poverty and social exclusion is one likely to achieve more by very targeted initiatives or by concentrating on broader efforts to reduce inequalities in society and to promote more universalist approaches which foster a wider support base in society and thus lead to more pressure for improvements?

6 The Swedish case: social security under reform[1]

Background

In the 1990s, the Swedish system of social security has been heavily challenged by a number of factors, economic as well as political. As a result, almost every area of the system is affected by ongoing reform. Some changes have already been implemented, other changes are in the process of being so, whereas changes in yet other programmes are still to be found at an early stage of the legislative process. However, the past years have taught us that we are in a volatile period, and towards the end of the day not all initiatives and proposals will actually be implemented.

It is hence difficult to predict the actual outcome of the reform work. Yet it should be possible to describe the nature of the proposals. The purpose of this paper is to outline the different types of action taken in the various branches of the social security system since the last (1994) election and to briefly examine the background, motives and nature of the measures taken. The study is restricted to the cash-benefit programmes.

In a way, the 1994 election campaign falsified standard public choice theory in the sense that the political parties were competing with programmes that were aimed at cutting benefits and/or increasing taxes. The Social Democratic party issued about a month before the election a programme which included a number of measures that were designed to deal with the rapidly increasing budget deficit and which included benefit cuts as well as tax increases. The proposals about benefit cuts were in some cases specified in terms of techniques, in other cases the amounts were specified. The overriding goal was to get control over the development of the public finances. To limit the damage of the expenditure cuts, there was an explicit priority to reduce expenditure on transfers and not on services since it was assumed that inadequate health care and child care might have irreversible effects on, for example, children's health and life chances, while cash benefits could be increased again if the public finances would be improved.

In government, the Social Democratic party has pursued very tough fiscal policies. Part of the strategy has been to increase a number of taxes, including social security contributions of the insured persons. This contributed to almost half of the improvement of the finances. The focus in the present paper is, however, on the changes to the other half, the benefit side. What is the nature of these changes? Is the Swedish model abandoned?

Swedish benefits in transition

Old-age pensions

In 1994, the Swedish parliament took a decision about 'guidelines' for the future of the public pension system. The decision was about the principles for the reform work of the old-age pensions and the actual legislation is yet to be worked out, although several parts of the new system have been subject to public review. It is anyway intended to only gradually phase out the old system. It is, therefore, a complicated

Joakim Palme, Swedish Institute of Social Research, Stockholm University, and Irene Wennemo, Swedish Trade Union Confederation.

task to comment on changes in the pension area because, on the one hand, there is this 'big' reform work concerning the long-term development of the system and, on the other hand, 'small' changes which concern the present system.

The 'big' pension reform represents both continuity and change with respect to the old system. The continuity is to be found in the underlying goal that a universal, publicly administered system should provide for both basic income and income replacement. The changes lie in the qualifying conditions, indexing of benefits, funding, and co ordination between the basic and earnings-related benefits. In the future, the earnings-related pensions will be shifted from a 'defined benefit' to a 'defined contribution' formula. However, it will continue to be a 'pay as you go' scheme, and the funding will be 'fictitious'. The system will be indexed to the development of real wages which means that the size of the pensions will follow the growth of the economy. It also means that the income ceiling for benefit purposes will be raised if real wages grow. This indicates that the present division of labour between the public and occupational programmes will be maintained.

The basic benefit will be paid only as a supplement for those with no or low earnings-related benefits. The earnings-related benefits will form the first tier of the pension systems in both countries, and the basic benefit will be used only as supplements. This shift will be a relatively small step for the individual pension recipient but in terms of policy principles it represents a big step. During autumn 1995, a heated debate was raised around the issue of whether occupational pensions should reduce

the size of the publicly provided basic benefit in Sweden (which actually was indicated by the guidelines). The political parties that stood behind the reform have recently agreed to leave the guaranteed basic benefit unaffected by all kinds of private pensions, occupational as well as individual.

A new element of the compulsory pension system is an individual and fully funded benefit to be based on contributions equivalent to 2 per cent of the gross wage. Since each individual is supposed to be able to take the decision about the placement and management of the funded contribution, this programme implies a shift of the control of pension funding from the public to the private sector.

The reform guidelines had been laid down as a compromise between the bourgeoisie parties and the Social Democrats. This is reflected in their content. Each of the parties to some extent had to abandon old views. The political commitment to a 'big state' in the provision of old-age pensions stands in clear contrast to the ideological commitments of the bourgeoisie parties to a 'small state'. It is likely that the parties to the right to an important degree were influenced by the fact that the old system had generated interests and expectations among large segments of their own electorates. It simply made it difficult to abandon the public commitment to secure old people's incomes on purely ideological ambitions. On the other hand, the Social Democrats had to make certain concessions. They had, for example, to abandon 'their' defined benefit plan (ATP) and they agreed to introduce the individual premium reserve programme with implications for the control of funding.

The scepticism within the Social Democratic

party towards the pension reform came to surface in connection with the 'extra party congress' which was held in March 1996 (as a consequence of Ingvar Carlsson's resignation from the chairmanship of the party). In the 'policy guidelines' for the party formulated by the congress, it was stated that the party will stick to the compromise but that it will organise a broad discussion within the party on the pension reform. Special attention will be given to the funding issue, especially since its introduction stands in conflict with the goals laid down in the 'convergence programme' which parliament has decided on with the ambition to meet the convergence criteria for EMU. The outcome of this discussion indicated that there was a lot of criticism towards some parts of the pension reform. However, during the ordinary party congress in September 1997, the Social Democratic party decided that it should stick to the five party compromise while pursuing an explicit Social Democratic line in finding solutions to the remaining 'technical issues' in the reform work.

Meanwhile, a number of decisions have been taken since the last election that are affecting both pensions spending and the earned pension rights. Expenditures have been affected primarily by changes in the indexing of benefits. As long as the budget deficit is high, benefits are not fully indexed which means that the benefits will lose in real value. A similar mechanism has been used to reduce the earned entitlements to future pensions. In a way, these decisions about the changes in the indexing of benefits have accomplished what would have been achieved automatically by the proposed indexing in the reformed system. In addition to the cuts in the ordinary pension benefits, a number of

measures have been taken to cut expenditures on the housing supplements for pensioners. These changes have removed some of the extreme marginal effects but also sharpened the income and wealth testing of the system.

Other changes have also affected the expenditures on pensions. One example is that married persons will receive the lower rate of the basic pension even when they are not married to another pensioner. Many individual pensioners have been affected by the expenditure cuts but as a collective the population above pension age has improved its situation, not least as a result of maturing earnings-related pensions – both public and occupational.

Early retirement benefits
As in all West European countries, early exit from the labour force has increased rather dramatically in Sweden over the past decades. This is likely to be an outcome of a complex process involving both changes in the labour market and in the social security system. In the 1990s, there have been changes in both these areas, as well as in other parts of the social security system, with consequences for the development of early retirement from the labour force.

In 1993, the number of new early retirement pensioners increased as a consequence of a strategy to pension those who were long-term recipients of sickness insurance benefits. This was followed by a decrease in the number of new early retirements in 1994, at the same time as the number of long-term sick went down further. Figures for 1995 point in the same direction. The trend of lower early retirement/long-term sickness thus seems to have persisted despite the continued high unemployment rate and persistently high long-term unemployment.

The size of benefits for early retirement pensioners has been affected by the same changes in indexing as old-age pensioners. The fact that the basic pensions for married persons are now paid at the same (and lower) rate, irrespective of whether they are married to another pensioner, has probably affected early retired persons more than old-age pensioners.

In addition, other measures have been taken with the specific purpose of reducing expenditures on early retirement. This was part of the election programme. The changes have concerned increased demands on the medical investigation and documentation of the work incapacity as well as the criteria according to which an early retirement benefit will be granted.

This will make the system a pure insurance for ill-health. As a result of the pension reform, the early retirement pensions will be transferred to the sickness insurance. At the beginning of 1997 a commission on the formation of the pension system for pre-retirement was set up. It is led by the former Social Insurance Minister, Anna Hedborg, who was one of the main architects behind the old-age pension reform. She was due to present a report on how the new early retirement pension should be designed in October 1997.

Unemployment benefit

The unemployment insurance system in Sweden differs from the rest of the social security system in the sense that the core programme is a voluntary, state-subsidised system administered by the trade unions. In addition there is a basic benefit, the right to which, however, is tied to quite strict qualifying conditions (but no means testing). The Conservative government reduced the replacement level to 80 per cent in 1993. They further introduced a compulsory clause in the core unemployment insurance. All those who had not joined any of the voluntary programmes were affiliated with a government equivalent. At the same time an insured person's social security contribution to unemployment insurance was introduced. Both these latter changes were removed as the Social Democratic party came into power in 1994.

Following the proposal of a reduction of the replacement level in sickness insurance which came in January 1995, there came a new proposal in the spring that reduced the replacement levels to 75 per cent as of 1 January 1996 in both sickness and unemployment insurance. This was heavily criticised by the unions. As part of the so-called 'Persson-plan', which was agreed on by the Social Democratic party and the Trade Union Confederation (LO) during the winter 1996, replacement levels are going to be increased to 80 per cent. This was coupled with changes in the requalification possibilities, meaning that it would no longer be possible to requalify for an unemployment insurance benefit infinitely by just taking part in training programmes and relief work.

In the beginning of 1997 the Minister of Labour Market Affairs presented a proposal on the formation of the unemployment insurance. It has gained support both from the LO as well as from the Centre party. The changes in the qualification conditions have become more modest, relative to the ones proposed earlier, but imply a strengthening related to the actual qualifying conditions. Beside the increase of the benefit level to 80 per cent from 27 September

1997, the benefit ceiling and the minimum level also have been modestly increased.

Work injury insurance

The work injury insurance went through a rather dramatic development during the 1980s. After a few critical court decisions, the 1977 legislation, based on a general work injury concept, was applied more liberally. The number of claims increased and the number of benefits which were paid out rose even more dramatically. This led to a big deficit building up in the work injury fund.

After 1987 the number of claims started to decrease as well as the rate of claims that were accepted but the fund was still running a big deficit. In 1993 the work injury concept was made stricter. The legislation demands a strong degree of probability before any benefits are paid out. Also, the co-ordination with sickness insurance benefit was made complete. It used to be that the work injury benefit (if the claim was accepted) was paid out at 100 per cent of past earnings. Now the benefit is the same unless the injury is permanent, when special supplements may be paid. The work injury benefit is presently under review in the parliamentary SAK committee (sickness-work-injury insurance committee).

Sickness cash benefit

The debate on sickness absenteeism was very heated towards the end of the 1980s. As a consequence the replacement levels for the first days of absence were reduced and a sick pay period of two weeks was introduced by a decision taken in 1990/91. The centre-right government tried to introduce two waiting days when they came into office. In connection with

the 1992 crisis agreement with the Social Democratic opposition, it was agreed to limit it to one waiting day. Both the sickness- and work-injury insurance programmes were supposed to be transferred to the partners of the labour market. However, the political willingness to pursue this shift was very weak. By March 1995, the SAK committee had received new directives which pointed to a continued universal public system.

Much debate during the winter of 1995 was centred around the issue of whether to keep the waiting day and the 80 per cent replacement level, or to reduce the replacement level to 75 per cent and abolish the waiting day. It ended with both 75 per cent and one waiting day. However, along with the increased replacement level for unemployment benefits, the sickness benefit is also paid at 80 per cent.

Following the downturn in the business cycle and the reductions in benefit levels sickness absence has gone down. This is likely to be an effect of both changing incentives and labour market conditions. A number of suggestions in this year's budget (as well as last year's) will reduce expenditures further.

Parental insurance

The parental insurance was introduced in 1974. The legislation entitled parents to six months' leave after the birth of the child and compensation for the income loss with 90 per cent of the previous income. Either the father or mother could stay at home during these six months. Sweden was the first nation to introduce a legislation that gave men equal rights to stay at home with the new-born child.

The leave period was increased gradually during the 1980s. By 1988 it had reached the length of 12 months with 90 per cent compensation and three months with a flat rate benefit level. In the election that year the Social Democrats declared that they were going to prolong the paid leave period further to 18 months. However, the economic recession and an unforeseen baby boom made the government back-off from its intention.

In 1994 the centre-right government introduced a change in the legislation. One month was reserved for the father and one for the mother. The purpose of this change was to increase fathers' use of parental leave. However, replacement levels were decreased to 80 per cent with the exception of the two reserved months when the compensation was still 90 per cent. The Conservative-led government abolished the three months with flat-rate benefit and introduced a care allowance to parents with children between one year and three years. The change was implemented in 1994, two months before the election. The care allowance was paid to mothers whose children did not use public child care. It was paid at a flat rate and was taxable. When the Social Democratic party got into power they abolished the care allowance and reintroduced the three months with a flat-rate benefit. From January 1996 the replacement level was reduced to 75 per cent and to 85 per cent for the two reserved months but in the last government a bill increased the replacement level to 80 per cent, while the higher benefit level for the two reserved months is to be abolished.

Child benefit

In 1990 and in 1991 the child benefit was increased substantially as a part of the implemented tax reform. The child benefit reached an all-time high since the introduction in 1948, both in real terms and relative to wages. Since then the nominal value of the child benefit has been stable which has implied a decrease in its real value. From 1996 the benefit level per child was reduced from 750 crowns to 640 crowns a month.

In 1982 a supplementary child benefit to large families was introduced. From the third child the benefit increased in size. The increase grew in size until the fifth child. The supplementary benefit grew in economic importance until 1989. Resources from the means-tested housing allowance were transferred to the universal support of large families. From 1994 the Conservative government lowered the support for large families by a decrease for families with five or more children. In 1995 the Social Democratic government followed by reducing the benefit to the third and fourth children. A decision was taken that the supplementary benefit to large families should be entirely abolished. However, families that had already attained the right to the benefit would be entitled to keep it until their children have grown up but for families with children born after 1 January 1996 no supplementary benefit was given. However, following decisions taken at the 1997 party congress, the Social Democratic government reversed the earlier cutbacks on child benefits in their 1997 autumn Budget which means that from January 1998 the child benefit will be paid at 750 crowns per month and the supplementary benefit for large families will be reintroduced.

Maintenance for children with non-cohabiting parents

Already by 1937, children who were living with

their unmarried mothers were supported by the state if their fathers did not fulfil their obligation to support them. This maintenance was later reclaimed from the father by the state. It was a system that functioned well for decades but started to be eroded in the 1970s and the 1980s. It gradually became easier to pay no, or very little, support to the child for the parent that did not live together with it. During the last years only a small part of the support has been reclaimed from the parents.

There are many different causes behind this development. However, the most important is not an unwillingness to pay. The parents pay a high share of the reclaimed maintenance. The problem has instead been that it has been very easy to get and keep a low maintenance level. The state has been responsible for a guaranteed level; if the maintenance level fell below this the state paid the difference. The new rules have been in force since February 1997. The maintenance is today related to the income level of the parent who does not live with the child. Neither the income of the parent who lives with the child nor that of a new spouse is taken into account. The guaranteed maintenance level is not changed, but the earlier indexing of it has been abolished.

Housing benefit

During the 1980s, the economic importance of housing allowances to families with children decreased markedly. When the tax reform was implemented in 1990–91 the housing allowances were made more generous. Simultaneously the subsidies to house building were reduced and rents increased markedly. As an effect of these changes the costs increased and the number of benefit recipients nearly doubled. Under the

Conservative government a new way of measuring income was introduced. It made it impossible to control the statements given by the beneficiaries and thereby the development of costs. A number of measures have been taken by the Social Democratic government in order to reduce costs (by 20 per cent). The most important change in the system is a new way of assessing income. The benefit will be set preliminarily through the use of income reports from the beneficiaries. Later the information will be controlled against the official tax records. If the taxed income exceeds the reported, the beneficiary has to pay back part of the benefit to the state. If the reported income exceeds the taxed income, the beneficiary will receive an additional benefit.

Moreover, the housing allowance is reduced for owner-occupiers. For dwellings and houses that exceed an upper limit in terms of square metres, the benefit is reduced. There are further changes for employers and self-employed, and for claimants with wealth. For spouses the income level for receiving full benefit will be assessed individually. This decreases the benefit for households where one of the spouses has no income and one of the spouses has an income exceeding the income level. The purpose of this change, besides reducing expenditures, is to decrease marginal effects for those who begin to work while receiving a housing allowance.

Social assistance

In Sweden, the municipalities are responsible for social assistance, including the level of benefits. However, there is also a national juridical minimum norm. If social assistance recipients are discontented with the decision in the municipality, they may appeal against it and become compensated for the difference between the municipal benefit and the national norm. In 1993 a commission proposed that there should be a national minimum scale rate determined by parliament.

The question of the social assistance level has gained much attention during recent years. In the recession in the early 1990s real wages decreased and the relative size of the social assistance norm increased since it is tied to the development of consumer prices. Another important factor for the relative increase in assistance levels is the rapid increase in housing costs which have affected consumer prices and, hence, social assistance levels. However, for social assistance recipients the housing costs are paid separately, and entirely, in addition to the standard rate.

In the beginning of 1997 it was decided that a national minimum should be implemented. The level was, however, lower than that proposed by the commission. The municipalities that have to pay out the assistance have been critical since they have little influence on the assistance level. They suggest that they should have full freedom to decide the level of social assistance.

Discussion

The 1990s have brought the Swedish social security system into a period of transition. Even if it is not the first time in post-war history that cutbacks have been attempted, it is the first time such measures have actually been implemented. When it comes to the changes over the past few years it is obvious that most of them have been triggered by an urgent need for cost control in order to stop the increasing budget deficit.

However, there are other motives too, and it would be misleading to see the changes only as devices to cut back on expenditure. In several cases it has been a question of dealing with, and hopefully reducing, unintended consequences of earlier reforms. In other instances changes have been made in order to adapt to a changing environment.

We can only speculate about the consequences of these changes. What complicates the picture in terms of income distribution is that a number of taxes have been increased and the rise in unemployment has decreased the importance of employment income. On the whole, quite surprisingly, the dramatic increase in unemployment has only marginally increased income inequalities. It appears that most of those who have become unemployed have been well protected by the unemployment insurance and social assistance recipiency is low in this category. However, it goes without saying that the cutbacks in the unemployment benefits as well as other support programmes have negatively affected the incomes of the unemployed persons and their households. It is also evident that the newcomers on the labour market, such as young persons and immigrants, have suffered economically from lost employment opportunities. As a result, the number of social assistance recipients has increased. Many individual old-age pensioners have been affected by the expenditure cuts but as a collective the population above pension age has improved its situation, not least as a result of maturing earnings-related pensions – both public and occupational. The biggest losers in terms of economic standards over the crisis period appear to be families with children. Their incomes have been affected by benefit cuts and tax increases as well as by reductions in earnings because of the increased unemployment.

When it comes to the design of the cuts, short-term and long-term goals have come into conflict. Sometimes the long-term goals have been given priority. Child benefits were reduced in nominal terms for the first time. This can be seen as a defensive strategy for the universal model of social policy. The alternatives would have changed the character of the programme. The risk with means testing is of course that the middle-class support is eroded in the long run, eventually leading to even lower child benefits. Moreover, means testing always sharpens the so-called poverty traps. This is also the case if child benefits are taxed, which has been another suggested alternative. A similar dilemma concerns sickness insurance. The decision to reduce benefit levels uniformly for all people at all income levels has been criticised for not being sensitive enough to the situation of low income earners. However, the alternative of reducing the income ceilings for benefit purposes would create a situation where very large segments of the labour force would have to shift their primary reliance from a public to an occupational programme. The maintenance allowance is an example of redesign intended to make the system work more as it was intended. In addition, it can also be seen as a way of sharpening the responsibility of parents to support their offspring economically. The lack of indexing can be seen as a long-term retrenchment strategy.

Despite all the cutbacks, it appears fair to conclude that the Swedish model of social security remains largely intact. The primary reliance is still on universal earnings-related programmes complemented by universal basic security benefits. The elements of voluntary, state-subsidised insurance are retained along with targeted and means-tested programmes. Yet the system of social security has been shaken by a number of factors. First, the cost explosion following the advent of mass unemployment in the early 1990s. Uncertainty, and lack of predictability, concerning the provision of social security benefits for the future have been replaced by a new kind of uncertainty. The great number of changes has to some extent eroded the public belief in the political commitment to the welfare state of the major political parties. Even if we do not wish to enter into the business of predicting the future of the Swedish welfare state it is interesting to note that the most important catalyst behind the changes over the past few years, the rapidly increasing budget deficit, will no longer work the way it has as the state will be running a surplus in the near future. Yet a reasonable assumption is that 'outside' factors, such as economic growth and the employment situation, will continue to play an important role. The critical 'within' factor has to do with the risks of an expansion of private insurance as a consequence of lower replacement rates in the statutory programmes. Such a development is likely to have repercussions on the political legitimacy and support of the welfare state in the electorate.

Note

1   This paper is based on a longer and fully referenced paper by the same authors with the title 'Swedish social security reform in the 1990s: reform and retrenchment', which

is available as CWR Working Paper 9, Centre for Welfare State Research (email cwr@smsfi.dk), The Danish National Institute for Social Research, Herulf Trolles Gade 11, DK-1052 Copenhagen, Denmark.

7 Trends in Poland, the Czech Republic, Slovakia, Hungary and Slovenia[1]

An overview of the system and present trends in separate countries

Over the last hundred years, the development of welfare state models in this region has been based on the Bismarckian tradition of social insurance linked primarily to employment. Pre-reform Central and Eastern Europe provided a safety net by combining full employment, generous family benefits and social insurance. Employment was guaranteed and, though wages were low, many basic requirements were provided free or at subsidised prices. There was no need for unemployment benefits or additional social protection. Apart from this, a generous set of family and maternity benefits was also provided which represented a major supplement to income (20 – 25 per cent). The motives for such provision were not solely those of an anti-poverty policy. They were also a way of providing a significant level of income support (Atkinson and Micklewright, 1992, pp. 214–19).

Poland

Social security schemes favour the employed in the 'state' sector and their families. The state monopoly of social insurance leaves no room for private initiative. In such a situation, social welfare is limited to assisting those who are unable to take care of themselves, such as the elderly and people with special needs. Pension insurance is controlled solely by the state, providing an old age, disability, and survivors' benefits on the basis of a 'pay-as-you-go' system. Family benefits developed extensively,

including family allowances, child support and maternity leave, which are either means-tested or flat-rate.

Up to the 1990s, unemployment insurance did not exist. When it was first introduced, it covered 70 per cent of previous earnings of the unemployed without an initial time limit. Since 1992, the increase in the unemployment rate has brought some limitation to these benefits, posing both a time limit (a year) and a benefit rate (36 per cent of the average wage). Social assistance is a benefit delivered on a national basis, aimed at the poor and at groups with special needs. Both the state and local authorities share the responsibility for its operation (Ksiezopolski, 1995).

The Czech Republic

Under socialism, access to welfare was not universal, as only the self-employed and farmers were included in social security schemes shortly before 1989. Nevertheless, like the neighbouring countries under consideration, it was a mix of universal elements and a strong work orientation. Residual forms of welfare in the sense of private charity and church involvement were weak (Vecernik in Marklund 1993, p. 109). Currently, income support schemes have the following set of properties.

The following are entitled to pensions: retired persons – men over 60 and women over 53 or 57 (depending on the number of children reared), the disabled, orphaned children, and widows and widowers.

Unemployment benefits are implemented by a special act; benefits go only to the registered

Dr Mojca Novak, University of Ljubljana, Slovenia.

unemployed. Benefits are means-tested – during the first three months, claimants receive 60 per cent of their average wage during the last three months of work; while during the last period of three months the entitlement drops to 50 per cent of the average wage of the unemployed. Those unemployed who participate in job-creation schemes, attending retraining programmes, receive higher benefits (70 per cent).

Low-income family support benefits are means-tested too, including family allowances and housing benefits. Some other benefits, such as parental benefits, soldiers' family benefits, and birth and death grants, are flat-rate.

Housing benefits are formally included in the family support scheme; they are means-tested and aim at financial assistance in either building or buying a house/flat (Kotynkova, 1996).

The major current social security issue, which is heatedly discussed in political circles, concerns the indexing and maintenance of the value of pensions to prevent impoverishment of the lowest income categories. The preservation of the real value of old-age pensions, particularly for those whose pension is the only income, has lately been brought into political focus, with claims that the ratio of the old-age pension to the average income will not change. Recently (1991), the basic pension has been estimated to be equivalent in value to between 20 per cent and 25 per cent of the national average income per head (Castle-Kanerova, 1992).

The Slovak Republic

The retirement scheme includes old age and disability pensions (full and partial), and pensions for widows, orphans, and widowers. The retiring age for men is 60 and for women 53 to 57, depending on the number of children brought up. The retired are entitled to a pension after 25 years of recorded work for men and 20 years for women. Those who suffer a severe decline of their work capability because of working in unhealthy conditions are entitled to a disability pension.

Unemployment benefits were established in early 1991. Initially, the longest period of the unemployment benefit entitlement was one year. The allowance depended on the average net wage during the last job and the amount was 65 per cent for the first six months of unemployment. Thereafter, it dropped to 60 per cent for the remaining (six) months. Since 1995, unemployment benefits have been lowered and paid according to the age of the job-seeker, so the older the job-seeker, the longer the entitlement for benefits, although this does not exceed the total period of nine months. Apart from this, benefits were also lowered – to 60 per cent for the period of the first three months and to 50 per cent for the rest of the period (up to nine months).

The family support scheme includes allowances supporting maternity and child rearing, such as child delivery support, child allowance (sick-leave is included too), and funeral contributions.

The housing policy includes financial assistance, aimed at building savings and loans. Any other support of tenants, such as housing cost subsidisation, is not yet legally regulated at present. This means that those who are unable to pay rent avoid paying it without sanctions (Radicova, 1996).

Hungary

Retirement: the 'pay-as-you-go' system is implemented according to a minimum pension and covers the majority of older people, even those who lack proper contribution (work) records. The replacement rate of pensions is relatively acceptable – between 60 per cent and 75 per cent – and the retirement age limit is low (55 and 60 years).

Family support schemes: in 1990 they became universal, but were also taxed. They include maternity leave and birth benefits, sick-leave, and means-tested allowances for mothers with three or more children under the age of ten (Ferge, 1995).

Slovenia

Since the establishment of the sovereign national state in 1991, Slovenia has undergone an in-depth renovation of social security legislation, aimed particularly at employment and unemployment, family support (including tax reduction for families), pension and disability insurance, social protection, and the minimum standard of living and health insurance.

Legally, all citizens and foreigners with special dispensations have equal access to income support if needy (disabled children and adults in different institutions). Individuals who are unable to work and those who are needy but able to work, like the long-term unemployed, are also entitled to these benefits in certain circumstances (having been means-tested). Individuals over the age of 60 who are fully unable to work are entitled to long-term social assistance without time limits. Short-term benefits (six months), may apply to those who

can prove their household income is below the official poverty line. Disabled people over the age of 18 are entitled to the flat-rate pensions.

Retirement: the current working life-span is 35 years (or the age of 55) for women and 40 years (or the age of 60) for men. Pensions are paid on a contributory basis. The pension is means-tested, so that its initial amount is assessed taking into account the ten best paid years from the work record. The amount of pension starts at 35 per cent of the average wage for men and 40 per cent for women for at least 15 years, with a proper work record, and can reach 85 per cent for the full insured period. Pensions are indexed monthly, according to the average wage, on a national basis. The pension of a breadwinner who has died is granted to family members such as a spouse and children, and also to parents, brothers and sisters, if they were dependent on the insured.

Disability pensions are granted for work injuries and other disabilities for a total loss of capacity, for remaining capacities that allow part-time work, and remaining capacities allowing full-time work at a different but frequently lower paid job. The pension depends on an assessment of the cause of disability, insured years, age, and old-age pension.

Unemployment: the unemployed are entitled to unemployment benefits and assistance by law. Benefits depend on the work record and are flat-rate (related to the average wage on the national level). The benefit period ranges from three months to two years. From then, the unemployed are entitled to unemployment assistance.

Child-care schemes which had been launched in the 1960s were transformed into low-income family support. The present scheme is financed by the state (80 per cent) and by local authorities (20 per cent), targeted at:

- children with special needs and other children, equipment for the new-born child, parental allowance (eligible for both parents subsequently), tax relief for the care of a sick family member

- providing and subsidising social services such as kindergartens, education, health care, vocational guidance, family consulting for parents and children separately, relief and services at home, and institutional service for individuals with special needs

- support for employed family members such as maternity leave (one year), sick-leave for a child, and compensation of income

- housing support, such as subsidised housing (state fund), subsidised rents (local level), and housing loans under favourable conditions.

Summing up, although some proposals and prepared programmes indicate the establishment of a three-tier pension system, a uniform public social security system operates in Slovenia at present. It includes health insurance, pension and disability insurance, and employment insurance. Social protection is provided by a social protection scheme and a family support scheme on a national basis. Social security funds are raised by contributions, while social protection operates according to a non-contributory principle.

Underlying trends and income exclusion

Central European countries under consideration experience similar demographic trends to Great Britain. These trends include increasing longevity, a higher proportion of elderly people and a decreasing proportion of the population in the labour force. Furthermore, the number of one-parent families is on the increase. Although survey results show the unemployment rate stabilising at approximately 10 per cent, the official data confirm a 15 per cent unemployment rate for the registered unemployed. In contrast to Great Britain, female employment has also stabilised at a rate of 45 per cent over the last 50 years. Furthermore, income support schemes are supposed to cover the whole population, but their rate is low.

Regardless of the number of unemployed in the household, the major dividing line in these countries is not between the 'work-rich' and the 'work-poor'. Hence, what counts is the level of income by which the household can meet its needs and aspirations. This is particularly the case since employed people without pay or with a pay rate which is too low are both common at present.

Policy trends and debates

The following common features of projected and gradually implemented reforms of social security in the countries under consideration (other than Slovenia) show retrenchment from initially generous entitlements:

- Unemployment was recently legally recognised and unemployment benefits were designed according to Western models. Although they were generous in the beginning, unemployment benefits have started to decrease in amount and duration.

- After harsh criticism from the international financial agencies that pensions are excessively generous, reforms have been launched in this sector too, implementing pension indexation, funding from contributions instead of from the budget, advocating of three-tier system (universal budget-funded pension, earnings-related pension and optional private scheme), and also establishing private occupational schemes.

- Family support schemes, which were employment-related, untaxed and favoured certain social groups (families with three and more children, single parents and children with special needs), have also undergone substantial reductions. Although they covered a substantial portion of children's needs, family allowances were criticised for being too high compared to Western countries, for being pro-natality oriented (third child) and for discriminating against the unemployed, because they are employment-related.

Part of the reforms aimed to correct these defects: family allowances became universal (Hungary), the monetary value of some benefits decreased and underwent certain time limitations (for students), they were taxed (in Hungary), better targeted (according to age of child, size of family), and means-tested (some universal benefits in Hungary and in the Czech Republic). The other major cash benefits relating to maternity and childhood have undergone indexation too, but some countries have also increased, for example, the universal birth grant, fully-paid maternity leave, an employment-related child-care grant that can be paid to both parents subsequently, and paid sick-leave for taking care of a sick child. Apart from this, a relatively well-developed network of child day care, including nurseries, kindergartens, school day-care centres, school meals and holiday homes, has also undergone a substantial decrease of facilities (Ferge, 1995).

References

Atkinson, A.B. and Micklewright, J. (1992) *Economic Transition in Eastern Europe and the Distribution of Income.* Cambridge: Cambridge University Press

Castle-Kanerova, M. (1992) 'Social policy in Czechoslovakia', in B. Deacon *et al.* (eds) *The New Eastern Europe: Social Policy Past, Present and Future.* London: Sage Publications, pp. 91–117

Ferge, Z. (1995) 'Social policy reform in post-Communist countries: various reform strategies, in S. Ringen and C. Wallace (eds) *Social Reform in East-Central Europe: New Trends in Transition.* Prague: Central European University, pp. 1–38

Kotynkova, M. (1996) 'Human dignity and social exclusion in the Czech Republic', paper

Ksiezopolski, M. (1995) 'Reforming the Polish social security system, in S. Ringen and C. Wallace (eds) *Social Reform in East-Central*

Europe: New Trends in Transition. Prague: Central European University, pp. 93–120

Marklund, S. (1993) 'Social policy and poverty in post-totalitarian Europe', *Scandinavian Journal of Social Welfare*, Vol. 2, pp. 104–14

Novak, M. (1996) 'Human dignity and social exclusion; country report on Slovenia', survey report

Radicova, I. (1996) 'Human dignity and social exclusion; the Slovak case', paper

Note

1   This text was prepared during the author's study stay in Wassenaar, at The Netherlands Institute for Advanced Study in the Humanities and Social Sciences (NIAS) of the Royal Academy of Arts and Sciences.

8 Income protection, inclusion and exclusion in the UK

An overview of the system and present trends

The UK system[1] of income protection can be characterised by four key features:

- An overarching national insurance scheme, devised by Beveridge. It originally paid flat-rate benefits in return for flat-rate contributions. It now pays mainly flat-rate benefits in return for earnings-related contributions.

- A set of 'universal' benefits which are neither contributory nor means-tested, that go automatically to people in certain situations, such as mothers with children or disabled people.

- A large role for means-tested (income-related) benefits, for families whose other income, including benefits, does not bring them above a basic threshold. Some means-tested benefits are available to people in low-paid work. The importance of means-tests has risen steadily, and they now account for nearly one-third of all benefit payments.

- A strong base of occupational pension schemes for those who have had well-paid long-term jobs. Government has encouraged people to move from the State Earnings Related Scheme to personal insurance policies.

Benefits are paid mainly to people in the four situations outlined below. An underlying social assistance scheme, Income Support, guarantees every non-working family a minimum income depending on its composition. Support for housing costs is described at the end of this section.

Retirement

Like almost all state benefits, the basic state pension has been frozen in real terms since the early 1980s, and has therefore declined relative to earnings. The State Earnings Related Pension Scheme, introduced in 1975 to augment the basic pension for those without adequate occupational schemes, is building towards maturity, but has already been curtailed. The state pension on its own does not always provide an adequate income, so 14 per cent of pensioners get income support, and as many as half are entitled to means-tested benefits.

Disability

A bewildering maze of benefits of which the most important elements are:

- *Incapacity Benefit:* an insurance-based scheme for those incapable of work. The rules have recently been tightened up in an attempt to stem an increase in claims and the level of payments has been reduced in many cases.

- *Disability Living Allowance:* a non-contributory and non-means-tested benefit, paid to people with restricted mobility or in need of care. A substantial increase in spending here means that the

Professor Richard Berthoud, University of Essex, and Donald Hirsch, international adviser to the Joseph Rowntree Foundation.

benefit is one of the few that has not been subject to political pressure.

Unemployment

Those with adequate contribution records get a flat-rate benefit, rather than an earnings-related one as in many European countries. This was limited to 12 months until recently; now only six months, after which only means-tested provision is available. The result is that only about one in five unemployed claimants now receive the insurance benefit, and a third of these have it topped up by Income Support. Benefits for the unemployed are paid at lower rates than those available to pensioners or disabled people.

The main policy response to the growth of unemployment has been to curtail benefits, and increase the pressure on unemployed people to show that they are actively seeking jobs. This is reflected in the new name for unemployment compensation: the 'Job-Seeker's Allowance'.

Families with children

Every mother in the country gets a flat-rate, tax-free Child Benefit payment for each child. But this is small relative to the extra cost of children assumed in means-test calculations. Out of work families with children therefore have to rely on Income Support.

Family Credit is available to couples with children or lone parents working at least 16 hours per week for low pay. It provides a minimum income in work above what would be available from Income Support, but is subject to a steep taper as earnings increase.

Twenty-five per cent of children in Britain live in families claiming Income Support and a further 10 per cent are affected by Family Credit.

There has been a substantial growth in the number of one-parent families and the majority of these claim Income Support. Recent policy initiatives have been intended to increase maintenance payments by fathers and encourage lone mothers to work.

Housing costs

A means-tested Housing Benefit is paid to tenants; it covers the entire rent of those claiming Income Support, and a proportion of the rent for those above the Income Support threshold, whether they are working or not. The cost has increased as more households are without work, and as rent levels have risen. A series of cuts in eligibility has aimed to reduce spending.

Householders on Income Support used to have their mortgage interest paid in full. This has been tightened up several times over the past few years, and the current complicated system means that new claimants will receive nothing at first and may have to wait up to nine months before the whole liability will be covered by social security. There is no means-tested mortgage benefit available to low-paid workers.

Figure 1 shows that spending on social security benefits has increased tenfold in real terms since the system was introduced in 1948. It has grown from 4 to 12 per cent of GDP in half a century.

Figure 2 shows that spending on all four of the categories of claimant reviewed above has increased since 1978, but especially for disabled people. The recent growth has been caused much more by increased numbers of claims, than by higher payments.

What is particularly striking (see Chapter 1,

Figure 1 Growth in real expenditure on social security, 1949–99

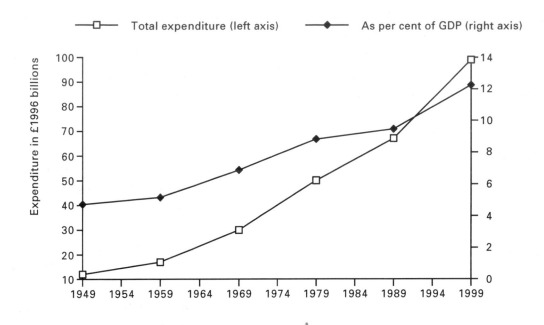

Figure 2 Real growth in spending on four types of claimant, 1978–99

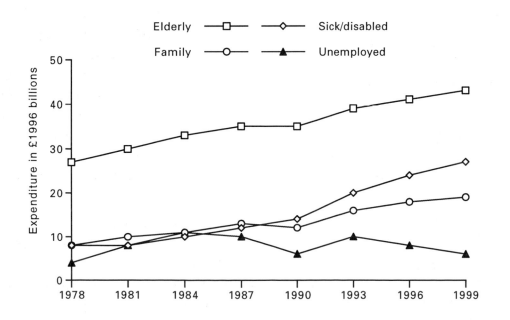

Figure 3) is the rise in means-tested benefits effectively for people on the poverty line.

The Conservative governments of 1979 to 1997 curbed but did not halt the long-term rise in the social security bill. But it was pushing for privatisation through greater individual responsibility – particularly in providing for old age. This applies not only to pensions but also to the cost of long-term care: it is hoped that many individuals will be able to insure themselves privately for this in future.

Underlying trends and income exclusion

Social and demographic trends

The following trends have had important effects on social security policy.

- *A rising number of elderly people,* which is increasing the dependency ratio. However, Britain has already passed through the worst of this trend and will face a relatively modest rise in this ratio in the twenty-first century.

- *A rise in the number of one parent families* which is blamed, in part, on the availability of benefits, though there is little direct evidence for this.

- *A growing number of married women in employment,* particularly part-time jobs. The benefit system was designed on the assumption of a male breadwinner and a female housekeeper, and caters poorly for part-timers.

- *A general increase in the categories of people who do not work* (including unemployed, lone parents, disabled) and a polarisation between work-rich (two earner) families

and work-poor (no earner) families. In 1993, the overall level of employment was almost the same as it had been in 1975. But the proportion of working-age adults living in workless households trebled over that period, from 5 to 15 per cent. This has been as important to the growth of social security spending as the ageing of the population.

- *Growing income inequality.* The proportion below half the national average increased from 9 per cent in 1979 to 24 per cent in 1993/94. The lowest 10 per cent of the population did not receive *any* increase in real income over that period, while the top 10 per cent increased their income by an amount more than double the total incomes of the poorest group.

Adequacy of benefit levels

Although the UK has an income safety-net in the form of Income Support, many would argue that those depending on it are excluded from adequate income. A huge volume of research has demonstrated that families living on social security benefits, especially Income Support, have a low standard of living and high levels of anxiety about money. It has often been argued that this is an unacceptable level of poverty, but there are also significant bodies of opinion taking the view that benefit levels are more than adequate.

Exclusion from the system

Some people fall through the Income Support safety net. The two biggest categories of excluded people, which overlap considerably, are the homeless and young people under 18. The number of literally roofless people has increased sharply in recent years. A high proportion of those wandering the streets with no home are under-18 year olds, who for the past decade have been excluded from claiming any support from the state other than in exceptional circumstances.

Policy trends and debates

Although need has been rising for the reasons outlined above, the government has tried to push down the proportion of national income spent by the state.

Pensions: public versus private

The post-war system of using today's insurance contributions to 'pay as you go' for today's pensions has come under fire. Future options being discussed include the privatisation and/or 'funding' of basic and/or second pensions. One problem is that during the transition to a 'funded' system – that is, one in which pensions are paid from the invested contributions of those who receive them – workers would have to contribute simultaneously to their parents' and to their own pensions. Another is that increased reliance on personal pension funds would lead to greater inequality in outcomes.

Means tests versus contingent benefits

Beveridge's original plan was for insurance entitlements to cover the overwhelming majority of risks, with social assistance available only as a safety-net. That has never been the case, in practice, and the role of means-tested benefits has expanded remorselessly. This is partly because of the growth of categories of claimant, such as lone parents and long-term unemployed, who are intrinsically difficult to

insure; and partly because of a political preference for limiting benefits to those in the greatest need. In the long run, though, means-tested benefits may be subject to the same political attack as has been launched on 'welfare' in the United States.

In-work benefits

There has been increasing emphasis on 'in-work' benefits: means-tested schemes designed to provide an incentive to take low-paid work. Family Credit has been fairly successful for lone parents, perhaps because part-time, low-paid work fits in well with mothers' other activities; but it has been less successful for couples with children. Disability Working Allowance, an equivalent benefit for disabled people, has had hardly any impact; Earnings Top-up (for single people and couples without children) is being tested in pilot schemes.

'Welfare to work'

A number of initiatives have been launched, and others have been proposed, to help individuals cross the boundary between claiming benefit and employment. These are designed to reduce the uncertainty associated with finding work, on the assumption that once people have re-entered the labour force they are likely to stay there.

Note

1 Great Britain and Northern Ireland have technically separate but almost identical social security systems. Many of the statistics quoted in this paper refer to Great Britain, rather than the United Kingdom as a whole.